MW01027018

Early Greek Thinking

Martin Heidegger

Works

Coeditors J. Glenn Gray
Colorado College

Joan Stambaugh
Hunter College of the City University of New York

By Martin Heidegger

Being and Time
Discourse on Thinking
The End of Philosophy
Identity and Difference
On the Way to Language
On Time and Being
Poetry, Language, Thought
What Is Called Thinking?
Early Greek Thinking

Early Greek Thinking

Martin Heidegger

Translated by
David Farrell Krell and Frank A. Capuzzi

Harper & Row, Publishers
New York, Evanston, San Francisco, London

Library of Congress Cataloging in Publication Data

Heidegger, Martin, 1889-
   Early Greek Thinking
   English translations of 4 essays. The Anaximander Fragment is the final essay of Holzwege; Logos, Moira, and Aletheia make up the third part of his Vorträge und Aufsätze.
   Includes bibliographical references.
   CONTENTS: The Anaximander Fragment.—Logos (Heraclitus, fragment B 50).—Moira (Parmenides VIII, 34-41).—Aletheia (Heraclitus, fragment B 16).
   1. Philosophy, Ancient—Addresses, essays, lectures.
I. Title.
B188.H44   180   74-6767
ISBN 0-06-063858-3

CONTENTS

Early Greek Thinking

TRANSLATORS' PREFACE

This book contains English translations of four essays written by Martin Heidegger between 1943 and 1954 on the matter of early Greek thinking. "The Anaximander Fragment" is the final essay of *Holzwege*, fourth edition (Frankfurt am Main: Vittorio Klostermann, 1963), pp. 296-343. "Logos," "Moira," and "Aletheia" make up the third part of *Vorträge und Aufsätze*, third edition (Pfullingen: Günther Neske, 1967), pp. 3-78. The German editions offer the following information:

Der Spruch des Anaximander. This piece is taken from a treatise composed in 1946. For criticism of Anaximander's text see also Friedrich Dirlmeier, "Der Satz des Anaximander v. Milet," *Rheinisches Museum für Philologie,* Vol. 87 (1938), 376-82. I agree with the delimitation of the text, if not the reasons given for it.

Logos. A contribution to the *Festschrift für Hans Jantzen,* edited by Kurt Bauch (Berlin, 1951), pp. 7 ff.; presented as a lecture to the Bremen Club on May 4, 1951; fully discussed in an unpublished lecture course in the summer semester of 1944 entitled "Logic."

Moira. An undelivered portion of the lecture course published as *Was heisst Denken?* (Tübingen: Max Niemeyer Verlag, 1954), with reference to pp. 146 ff. [Cf. *What Is Called Thinking?*, translated by Fred D. Wieck and J. Glenn Gray (New York: Harper & Row, 1968), pp. 240-44.]

Aletheia. A contribution to the *Festschrift* in honor of the 350th anniversary celebration of the Humanistic Gymnasium in Constance; first delivered in an unpublished lecture course on Heraclitus in the summer semester of 1943.

A glossary at the end of the book lists our attempts to translate the most difficult (usually the most important) terms. While we have checked one another's work, David Krell is responsible for the translations of the first two articles, Frank Capuzzi for the last two. Dr. Krell is responsible for the footnotes.

We would like to thank John Sallis and Reiner Schürmann of

Duquesne University, Bruce Foltz, Annabel Learned, Sherry Gray, D.S. Carne-Ross, and the series editors, Joan Stambaugh and J. Glenn Gray, whose efforts have resulted in innumerable substantial improvements in the translations. Thanks also to M. Salomé and Eunice Farrell Krell for help in preparing the volume. We hope readers will trouble themselves to forward any corrections, suggestions, and comments to us, in care of the publisher.

D. F. K.
F. C.

INTRODUCTION

by David Farrell Krell

In "The Anaximander Fragment" Heidegger remains preoccupied with the problem of translation. Before we do any actual translating, he says, we must translate *ourselves* to what a fragment says, what it is *thinking;* we must first arrive on its foreign shores and, like Hermes on Ogygia, stop to contemplate before we can return with some fitting memento of it to the land of our own language.

Without philological aids of all kinds Dr. Capuzzi and I could never have ventured our own translation. Even with those aids and with the unstinting help of learned friends there can be no guarantee that we have made the trip as it ought to be made. Whether our translation thoughtfully brings to the English language what Heidegger contemplates on archaic Greek shores, whether it is hermeneutically circumspect, whether it remains receptive of the matter for thinking: these questions give us pause at the end of our labors which only critical and generous readers can answer. We have tried to be literal, tried harder to be faithful. We can only gesture toward the glossary at the end of the book, as though that were apologia enough.

"The Anaximander Fragment" is the last essay of the book Heidegger calls *Woodpaths* (*Holzwege:* the French edition translates *Chemins qui mènent nulle part*). At the beginning of the book the following lines appear:

"Wood" is an old name for forest. In the wood are paths which mostly wind along until they end quite suddenly in an impenetrable thicket.

They are called "woodpaths."

Each goes its peculiar way, but in the same forest. Often it seems as though one were like another. Yet it only seems so.

Woodcutters and forest-dwellers are familiar with these paths. They know what it means to be on a woodpath.

By the time the reader has arrived at "The Anaximander Fragment" he will have gone the way of a reflection on art, "The Origin of the Art Work"; on modern science and the Cartesian philosophy, "The Age of the World View"; on Hegel's Introduction to *The Phenomenology of Spirit*, "Hegel's Concept of Experience"; on the essence of nihilism, "The Word of Nietzsche: God is Dead"; and on the role of poets in the epoch of nihilism, "Wozu Dichter?"[1] Only after a series of reflections on art, poetry, and modern and contemporary philosophy does Heidegger broach the subject of this early fragment of thinking ascribed to Anaximander of Miletus. Only after these turns in the path does he attempt a translation to early Greek thinking.

"Logos," "Moira," and "Aletheia" constitute the third and final part of Heidegger's *Lectures and Essays (Vorträge und Aufsätze:* the French edition translates *Essais et Conférences).* The Foreword to all three parts reads:

So long as it lies before us unread, this book is a collection of lectures and essays. For the reader it might lead to a gathering which would no longer need to bother about the individual aspects of each piece. The reader might see himself conducted along a path, preceded by an author who, since he is an *auctor*, will if all goes well dispense an *augēre*, an enrichment, and bring matters to a fruitful outcome.

In the present case we would do better to toil as much as we ever have, so that unrelenting efforts may prepare a region for what since ancient times is to-be-thought but is still unthought. From the open space of such a region a thinking might try to address what is unthought.

If he were such a toiler an author would have nothing to express and nothing to communicate. He wouldn't wish to stimulate anyone, because those who have been stimulated are already sure of what they know.

If everything turns out for the best, an author on paths of thinking can only point the way [*weisen*] without being himself a wise man [*ein Weiser*] in the sense of σοφός.

1. The first and last appear in M. Heidegger, *Poetry, Language, Thought*, trans. Albert Hofstadter (New York: Harper & Row, 1971). See also his *Hegel's Concept of Experience* (New York: Harper & Row, 1970).

Thoughtpaths, which are indeed past when one has passed by them
—although for one who has been going on them they persist in coming—wait.
They wait until some time in thinking they go. While usual technical-
representational thinking, technical in the broadest sense, forever wills to go
forward and tears ahead of everything, paths which point out a way occasionally
open upon a view of a solitary sheltered clearing [*ein einziges Ge-birg*].

Without listing the titles of all the lectures and essays which lead
to those on early Greek thinking, we might glance over our shoulders
along the path already indicated. Heidegger speaks of technology and
science, about will to power and the overcoming of metaphysics; he
reflects on Nietzsche's *Zarathustra;* he asks "What is called thinking?"
and ponders the meaning of building and cultivating, dwelling and
thinking, of "things," and of Hölderlin's line ". . . poetically man
dwells. . . ." Only then do we hear of "Logos," "Moira," "Aletheia." A
proper introduction to these three lectures and to the Anaximander
essay would be a reflection which had traveled all the earlier stretches
of the path and still could see the forest as well as the trees. It could do
this only by catching a glimpse of the clearing Heidegger calls *das
Selbe,* τὸ αὐτό, the Same.

Four fragments of early Greek thinking dominate Heidegger's
thoughts in the present collection. Each is a truncated monument of
thinking. Like the torso of a river god or the temple of Poseidon at
Sounion, each fragment conveys a sense of loss, of tragic withdrawal
and absence; yet each is a remnant of an exhilarating presence. These
four fragments are ascribed respectively to Anaximander (B 1), Heraclitus (B 50), Parmenides (B VIII, 34-41), and again Heraclitus (B 16).
We can read English versions of the standard German translations by
Hermann Diels and Walther Kranz in a minute's time.

1. But where beings have their origin there also their passing away occurs,
   according to necessity; for they pay recompense and penalty to each other
   for their injustice, according to the assessment of time.

2. Listening not to me but to the Logos, it is wise to say, in accordance with
   the Logos: all is one.

3. Thinking and the thought "it is" are the same. For without the being in

relation to which it is uttered you cannot find thinking. For there neither is nor shall be anything outside of being, since Moira bound it to be whole and immovable. For that reason all these will be mere names which mortals laid down, convinced that they were true: coming-to-be as well as passing away, Being as well as non-being, and also change of place and variation of shining colors.

4. How can one hide himself before that which never sets?[2]

Origin and decay, time and necessity, the word and the One, Being and thinking, a sun that never sets: it will take us more than a minute to consider what these fragments say or even what they are talking about, and whether they have anything in common with one another and with us. If we find these matters puzzling and impenetrable we are certainly not the first.

The men who raised these monuments were already "renowned and venerable" by Plato's time. When in Plato's *Sophist* (241d 3,5) the Eleatic Stranger questions the views of "father Parmenides" he takes care lest his probing transform him into a sort of parricide. If the eccentric Heraclitus receives a more polemical treatment in Plato's hands it is perhaps because the Ephesian's thought is as provocative as it is elusive. Whatever reservations Plato may have made with respect to his predecessors' views he is always ready to concede *that the matter of their thinking is difficult* (cf. *Soph.*, 243a-b). But what is difficult for the master can hardly be easy for the pupil.

After surveying the opinions of early thinkers from the point of view of his theory of causes, Aristotle (*Met.* II-a) suggests that investigation of the truth is both easy and difficult. Every investigator manages to reveal a part of it, while none can grasp the whole. In the same place Aristotle mentions a second and more serious difficulty, "the cause of which is not in the matter (πράγμασιν) but in us; for as

2. See Diels-Kranz, *Die Fragmente der Vorsokratiker*, 6th ed. (Berlin: Weidmannsche Verlagsbuchhandlung, 1951), I, 89, 161, 238, and 155. Cf. the translations by G. S. Kirk and J. E. Raven, *The Presocratic Philosophers: A Critical History with a Selection of Texts* (Cambridge, Eng.: The University Press, 1966), pp. 117, 188, and 277. (Kirk and Raven do not print Heraclitus B 16.) Cf. also the translation of Diels-Kranz by Kathleen Freeman, *Ancilla to the Pre-Socratic Philosophers* (Cambridge, Mass.: Harvard University Press, 1966), pp. 19, 28, 44, and 16. We have offered our own translations of the Greek texts, based on those of Diels-Kranz, throughout this volume.

the eyes of bats are to the blaze of day, so is the mind of our soul to things which are by nature most manifest of all" (*Met.*, 993b 9-11).

But who ridicules the bat for his blindness? *To whom* are the πράγματα most manifest? Genesis and collapse, necessity and time, one and many, being and thinking: if these shine like a sun that never relents, whose brilliance blinds, what are *we* to see in them?

What do the fragments say? Of what do they speak? We have no trouble with the first question until we take the second seriously. Only indirectly do the fragments indicate their subject matter, in the words τοῖς οὖσι, τὰ πάντα, ἔμεναι, τὸ ἐόν: things or beings, everything, to be, Being. These merest fragments of thought seem to talk about *everything*, all *being*, whatever *is*. We moderns are convinced that this is nonsense: one cannot talk about everything in general without uttering generalities or even "overgeneralizations." We are astounded by the Greeks' presumption. We refuse to talk that way. Being—*écrasez l'infame!* The history of *philosophy* becomes a nightmare from which we, Dedalus-like, are trying to awake. But indignant refusal and consignment to oblivion are hardly signs of wakefulness. Besides, we cannot entirely shake off the suspicion that this question of Being involves us rather intimately: we who raise the question are among the beings which—for a time—are.

Two forms of the word *Being* are especially widespread in Greek philosophical literature, τὸ ὄν and τὰ ὄντα. Both are substantive-participial forms whose articles suggest respectively the singular and plural neuter nominatives. Because of the nominative plural ending −τα, the second, which has been farther declined than the first, seems more "substantial." However, both devolve from εἰμί, εἶναι (I am, to be).[3] In the Ionian and Aeolian dialects, and therefore in epic usage, τὸ ὄν and τὰ ὄντα appear as τὸ ἐόν and τ'ἐόντα. Homer, Alcaeus, Sappho, Heraclitus, and Parmenides are among the many poets and thinkers of the eastern Hellenic territories where this form—which retains the verbal root *epsilon*—is employed. The Liddell and Scott Greek-English lexicon translates Plato's usage of τὸ ὄν and τὰ ὄντα

3. See M. Heidegger, *An Introduction to Metaphysics*, trans. Ralph Manheim (Garden City, N. Y.: Doubleday & Co., Anchor Books, 1961), chap. 2, "On the Grammar and Etymology of the Word 'Being.' "

respectively as "Being" and "the world of things," the German lexicons as *Sein* (Being) and *das Seiende* (beings). Of course, Plato's "world of things" is neither a world (κόσμος) nor is it of "things" (πράγματα, χρήματα); rather, it is a domain of beings called εἴδη. These are opposed to non-being or that which is not, μὴ ὄν, and are taken to be that which truly is. Τὰ ὄντα comes to mean "truth" and "reality." Herodotus already uses the word (in its Ionian form) in this way: he says κατὰ τὸ ἐόν, πᾶν τὸ ἐόν, and τὸ ἐόντα λόγον λέγειν, meaning "to tell the whole story in accordance with the way things truly are."

But the very first meaning for τὰ ὄντα listed by the lexicon is: "the things which actually [in the sense of the French *actuellement*] exist, the present, as opposed to the past and the future." Being is what is (at) present. In English, "present" can mean what *now* is, as opposed to what was before or later will be; or it can mean what is *here*, as opposed to what is somewhere else, hence absent. German says *die Gegenwart* for the first, *die Anwesenheit* for the second. The Greek words for Being suggest at once presence in time and place. What is most thought-provoking for Heidegger is the *coming to presence* of whatever presents itself, the Being of beings, the ἐόν of ἐόντα.

"The Anaximander Fragment" designates Being as presencing and introduces the themes which dominate Heidegger's study of the Greeks: Λόγος, the unique gathering of beings which language is; Μοῖρα, the fateful apportionment of Being in which the ontological difference—the difference between present beings and their presencing—is obliterated for Western thinking; Ἀλήθεια, the uncon- cealment of beings and concealment of Being. The temporary abate- ment of the waters of Lethe, the history of Being's fate or destiny *(das Geschick des Seins),* and the decisive role language plays in both, indicate what is singular about early Greek thinking, that is, the way in which beings manifest themselves as being *present.* The Being of be- ings is therefore taken for granted as the *presencing* of what presents itself. It is also decisive that the Greeks never did or could *think through* the meaning of presencing and establish it in and for the history of thought. By the time a philosophical literature develops, the meaning of ἐόν has receded to the threshold of oblivion. Soon it crosses that threshold: Being is reduced to one being among others, becomes itself a present entity which is variously named ἰδέα, ἐνέργεια, *actus purus*, reason, will, and will to power. Usually this figure is called the *supreme* being, as if by way of consolation; often it is simply called "God." But not in the last case.

From *Being and Time* (1927) to *Time and Being* (1962) Heidegger has sought to retrieve the meaning of τὸ ὄν and to think the Same as the nexus of temporality and Dasein, as the luminous clearing and concealing of Being, and as the event which engages man to the presencing of whatever is present. From first to last the nexus has been a tragic one. In "The Anaximander Fragment" Heidegger says that the essence of tragedy can be thought only in relation to the coming-to-presence of beings, since presencing implies approach *and* withdrawal, emergence *and* evanescence, rise *and* fall. Mortals share in the tragic essence in a peculiar way. At the end of "Moira," death is called the uttermost possibility of mortal Dasein *and* the innermost possibility which gathers and secures all disclosure of Being. One of the central issues of "Logos" becomes the need for mortals to become fit for their allotment (Μοῖρα) and not to mistake their participation in the Λόγος as some sort of conquest of mortality. For that would be hubris—more destructive than a holocaust, and sooner to be extinguished.

To recapture the tragic essence of early Greek thinking is an undertaking in which Heidegger joins Nietzsche. Nietzsche's description of the "philosopher of tragic insight," the thinker he locates before Plato, perhaps near the figure of Heraclitus, might suit Heidegger himself.

The philosopher of tragic insight [*Erkenntnis*]: He restrains the uncontrolled drive toward knowledge, but not through a new metaphysics. He does not set up a new faith. He feels the vanishing of the metaphysical ground as a tragic event and cannot find a satisfying compensation for it in the motley spiralling of the sciences. . . .[4]

Nietzsche calls the disappearance of ontological ground "the death of God" and calls for the liberation of τὰ ὄντα from the burden imposed on them by the shade of the dead God—the traditional λόγος of West-

---

4. Cited from Nietzsche's *Nachlass* by Marianne Cowan in her Introduction to F. Nietzsche, *Philosophy in the Tragic Age of the Greeks*, trans. Marianne Cowan (Chicago: Henry Regnery, 1962), p. 16.

ern metaphysics and morals. "The world of things" must once again be thought in terms of Aion, the child at play. But the experience of Aion, "this transformation of the Dionysian into a philosophical pathos," is an exercise in "tragic wisdom": Nietzsche utters his truth and goes down with it, since the death of God means the failure of dogmatic λόγος and the death of man.[5]

Nietzsche closes the ring of metaphysical enquiry into τὸ ὄν and brings metaphysics to its end, the exhaustion of its final possibility, by turning back to the beginnings of Greek philosophy. Whether or not Nietzsche's turning remains determined by Plato—or by one interpretation of Plato, namely Platonism—it is in Heidegger's view historic and fateful, for it marks the end of an epoch of Being.[6] In his *Introduction to Metaphysics* (p. 30), focusing on the question of the meaning of τὸ ὄν, Heidegger describes his own task as one of "bringing Nietzsche's accomplishment to a full unfolding." That means following Nietzsche's turn toward early Greek thinking in such a way as to bring the possibilities concealed in ἐόν to a radical questioning.

Thus the turning of Heidegger's own thought must be seen, not as some sort of development or shift in point of view, but as that moment in the eschatology of Being when the metaphysical sense of Being reaches its consummation and goes under. In the turning of its outermost gyre, thinking catches sight of remnants of thought which lie concealed in the beginning of the history of Being's destiny. Today these possibilities appear as fragments of early Greek thinking. They have not yet gone down; nor have they yet been heard.[7] We cannot hide ourselves from the matter contained in these fragments, since what they say or do not say to Plato and Aristotle, and through them to the Schoolmen and to all modern science and philosophy, shapes our thoughts about Being and man. These in turn determine the character of our world. Heidegger suggests that the *achèvement* of Occidental

5. F. Nietzsche, *Werke*, 3 vols., ed. Karl Schlechta (Munich: C. Hanser Verlag, 1954), III, 1,111; III, 376. Cf. his *Philosophy in the Tragic Age*, pp. 61-63. See also M. Heidegger, *Nietzsche*, 2 vols. (Pfullingen: G. Neske Verlag, 1961), I, 314, 333-34; Eugen Fink, *Spiel als Weltsymbol* (Stuttgart: Kohlhammer, 1960); and David Krell, "Towards an Ontology of Play," *Research in Phenomenology*, II, 63-93, esp. 67 ff.

6. Heidegger, *Nietzsche*, I, 464 ff.

7. See M. Heidegger, "Hegel und die Griechen," *Wegmarken* (Frankfurt/Main: V. Klostermann Verlag, 1967) p. 272.

philosophy is the expanding planetary dominion of technology. Given such a turn of affairs—and who could have predicted the way the history of metaphysics has turned out?—we come to face the matters raised in the fragments: rise and fall, time and its uses, language and the One, thinking and Being, illumination and concealment.

At the *end* to arrive at *early* Greek thinking: there is something distressing—even violent—in such a turnabout. Certainly it would be naïve to regard the present book as an introductory volume on early Greek philosophy. Although Heidegger takes each word of the fragments seriously—rather *because* he does so—his thinking plies a dangerous, uncharted course which we are at pains to follow. The violence of interpretation is unavoidable; no footnote can ameliorate it. But it is the violence inherent in any attempt to cross over to that foreign shore, the violence by which we overcome inertia and translate ourselves to the matter of early Greek thinking. If it is violent to insist that this matter casts significant light on contemporary problems, from the history of metaphysics and nihilism to the essence of technology, then Heidegger is surely violent. He demands that the fragments be rescued from the Museum for Historic Oddities and restored to their proper milieu: *thinking.* He insists that the fragments occupy contemporary man's contemporary reflection. *Early Greek Thinking* is not an idyll for weary men who would, like Hamlet's crab, go backward.

The path which leads us forward to the realm of early Greek thinking is celebrated in a fragment of a hymn by Friedrich Hölderlin called "Greece." By way of introduction we offer several lines, some from its beginning, some from its never-completed end.

Griechenland
(Dritte Fassung)

O ihr Stimmen des Geschicks, ihr Wege des Wanderers!
. . . Viel sind Erinnerungen . . .
Süss ists . . . unter hohen Schatten von Bäumen

11

Und Hügeln zu wohnen, sonnig, wo der Weg ist
Gepflastert zur Kirche. Reisenden aber, wem,
Aus Lebensliebe, messend immerhin,
Die Füsse gehorchen, blühn
Schöner die Wege, wo das Land—[8]

8. *Hölderlin Werke und Briefe* (Frankfurt/Main: Insel Verlag, 1969) I, 239-40. Lines 1, 9, and 46-51 are cited here.

Greece
(third draft)

O voices of destiny sent, you wanderer's ways!
. . . Many are the memories . . .
It is sweet . . . to dwell under high shadows
Of trees and hills, sunny, where the path is
Paved to church. But to travelers,
To him whose feet, from love of life,
Measuring always ahead, obey him,
More beautifully bloom those paths where the land—

ONE

The Anaximander Fragment

It is considered the oldest fragment of Western thinking. Anaximander reportedly lived on the island of Samos from the end of the seventh century to the middle of the sixth.

According to the generally accepted text the fragment reads:

ἐξ ὧν δὲ ἡ γένεσίς ἐστι τοῖς οὖσι καὶ τὴν φθορὰν εἰς ταῦτα γίνεσθαι κατὰ τὸ χρεών· διδόναι γὰρ αὐτὰ δίκην καὶ τίσιν ἀλλήλοις τῆς ἀδικίας κατὰ τὴν τοῦ χρόνου τάξιν.

Whence· things have their origin, there they must also pass away according to necessity; for they must pay penalty and be judged for their injustice, according to the ordinance of time.

Thus translates the young Nietzsche in a treatise completed in 1873 entitled *Philosophy in the Tragic Age of the Greeks.* The treatise was published posthumously in 1903, thirty years after its composition. It is based on a lecture course Nietzsche offered several times in the early 1870's at Basel under the title, "The Preplatonic Philosophers, with Interpretation of Selected Fragments."

In the same year, 1903, that Nietzsche's essay on the Preplatonic philosophers first became known, Hermann Diels' *Fragments of the Presocratics* appeared. It contained texts critically selected according to the methods of modern classical philology, along with a translation. The work is dedicated to Wilhelm Dilthey. Diels translates the Anaximander fragment in the following words:

But where things have their origin, there too their passing away occurs according to necessity; for they pay recompense and penalty to one another for their recklessness, according to firmly established time.

The translations by Nietzsche and Diels arise from different intentions and procedures. Nevertheless they are scarcely distinguishable. In many ways Diels' translation is more literal. But when a translation is only literal it is not necessarily faithful. It is faithful only when its terms are words which speak from the language of the matter itself.

More important than the general agreement of the two translations is the conception of Anaximander which underlies both. Nietzsche locates him among the Preplatonic philosophers, Diels among the Presocratics. The two designations are alike. The unexpressed standard for considering and judging the early thinkers is the philosophy of Plato and Aristotle. These are taken as the Greek philosophers who set the standard both before and after themselves. Traversing Christian theology, this view becomes firmly entrenched as a universal conviction, one which to this day has not been shaken. In the meantime, even when philological and historical research treat philosophers before Plato and Aristotle in greater detail, Platonic and Aristotelian representations and concepts, in modern transformations, still guide the interpretation. That is also the case when attempts are made to locate what is archaic in early thinking by finding parallels in classical archaeology and literature. Classic and classicist representations prevail. We expatiate on archaic logic, not realizing that logic occurs for the first time in the curriculum of the Platonic and Aristotelian schools.

Simply ignoring these later notions will not help in the course of translating from one language to another, if we do not first of all see how it stands with the matter to be translated. But the matter here is a matter for thinking. Granted our concern for philologically enlightened language, we must in translating first of all think about the matter involved. Therefore only thinkers can help us in our attempt to translate the fragment of this early thinker. When we cast about for such help we surely seek in vain.

In his own way the young Nietzsche does establish a vibrant rapport with the personalities of the Preplatonic philosophers; but his interpretations of the texts are commonplace, if not entirely superficial, throughout. Hegel is the only Western thinker who has thoughtfully experienced the history of thought; yet he says nothing about the

Anaximander fragment. Furthermore, Hegel too shares the predominant conviction concerning the classic character of Platonic and Aristotelian philosophy. He provides the basis for the classification of the early thinkers as Preplatonic and Presocratic precisely by grasping them as Pre-Aristotelians.

In his lectures on the history of Greek philosophy, at the point where he indicates the sources for our knowledge of this primeval epoch of philosophy, Hegel says the following:

Aristotle is the richest source. He studied the older philosophers expressly and with attention to fundamentals. Especially at the beginning of the *Metaphysics* (though in many other places besides) he spoke as a historian about the entire group of them. He is as philosophical as he is learned; we can depend on him. For Greek philosophy we can do nothing better than take up the first book of his *Metaphysics*. (*Works*, XIII, 189)

What Hegel recommends here to his listeners in the first decades of the nineteenth century had already been followed by Theophrastus, Aristotle's contemporary, his student, and the first successor to the leadership of the Peripatetics. Theophrastus died about 286 B.C. He composed a text with the title Φυσικῶν δόξαι, "the opinions of those who speak of φύσει ὄντα." Aristotle also calls them the φυσιολόγοι, meaning the early thinkers who ponder the things of nature. Φύσις means sky and earth, plants and animals, and also in a certain way men. The word designates a special region of beings which, in both Aristotle and the Platonic school, are separated from ἦθος and λόγος. For them φύσις no longer has the broad sense of the totality of being. At the outset of Aristotle's thematic observations on *Physics*, that is, on the ontology of the φύσει ὄντα, the kind of being called φύσει ὄντα is contrasted with that of τέχνῃ ὄντα, Φύσει ὄντα is that which produces itself by arising out of itself; τέχνῃ ὄντα is produced by human planning and production.

When Hegel says of Aristotle that he is "as philosophical as he is learned," this actually means that Aristotle regards the early thinkers in the historical perspective, and according to the standard, of his own *Physics*. For us that means: Hegel understands the Preplatonic and Presocratic philosophers as Pre-Aristotelians. After Hegel a twofold opinion concerning philosophy before Plato and Aristotle ensconces itself as the general view: (1) the early thinkers, in search of the first beginnings of being, for the most part took nature as the object of their representations; (2) their utterances on nature are inadequate approximations compared to the knowledge of nature which in the meantime had blossomed in the Platonic and Aristotelian schools, the Stoa, and the schools of medicine.

The Φυσικῶν δόξαι of Theophrastus became the chief source for manuals of the history of philosophy in Hellenistic times. These manuals prescribed the interpretation of the original writings of the early thinkers which may have survived to that time, and founded the subsequent doxographical tradition in philosophy. Not only the content but also the style of this tradition made its mark on the relation of later thinkers—even beyond Hegel—to the history of thought.

About 530 A.D. the Neoplatonist Simplicius wrote an extensive commentary on Aristotle's *Physics.* In it he reproduced the Anaximander fragment, thus preserving it for the Western world. He copied the fragment from Theophrastus' Φυσικῶν δόξαι. From the time Anaximander pronounced his saying—we do not know where or when or to whom—to the moment Simplicius jotted it down in his commentary more than a millennium elapsed. Between the time of Simplicius' jotting and the present moment lies another millennium-and-a-half.

Can the Anaximander fragment, from a historical and chronological distance of two thousand five hundred years, still say something to us? By what authority should it speak? Only because it is the oldest? In themselves the ancient and antiquarian have no weight. Besides, although the fragment is the oldest vouchsafed to us by our tradition we do not know whether it is the earliest fragment of its kind in Western thinking. We may presume so, provided we first of all think the essence of the West in terms of what the early saying says.

But what entitles antiquity to address us, presumably the latest latecomers with respect to philosophy? Are we latecomers in a history now racing towards its end, an end which in its increasingly sterile order of uniformity brings everything to an end? Or does there lie concealed in the historical and chronological remoteness of the fragment the historic proximity of something unsaid, something that will speak out in times to come?

Do we stand in the very twilight of the most monstrous transformation our planet has ever undergone, the twilight of that epoch in which earth itself hangs suspended? Do we confront the evening of a night which heralds another dawn? Are we to strike off on a journey to this historic region of earth's evening? Is the land of evening* only now emerging? Will this land of evening overwhelm Occident and Orient alike, transcending whatever is merely European to become the location of a new but primordially fated history? Are we men of today already "Western" in a sense that first crystallizes in the course of our passage into the world's night? What can all merely historiological philosophies of history tell us about our history if they only dazzle us with surveys of its sedimented stuff; if they explain history without ever thinking out, from the essence of history, the fundamentals of their way of explaining events, and the essence of history, in turn, from Being itself? *Are* we the latecomers we are? But are we also at the same time precursors of the dawn of an altogether different age, which has already left our contemporary historiological representations of history behind?

Nietzsche, from whose philosophy (all too coarsely understood) Spengler predicted the decline of the West—in the sense of the Western historical world—writes in "The Wanderer and His Shadow" (1880), "A higher situation for mankind is possible, in which the Europe of nations will be obscured and forgotten, but in which Europe will *live on* in thirty very ancient but never antiquated books" (Aphorism no. 125).

All historiography predicts what is to come from images of the past determined by the present. It systematically destroys the future and our historic relation to the advent of destiny. Historicism has today not only not been overcome, but is only now entering the stage of its expansion and entrenchment. The technical organization of communications throughout the world by radio and by a press already limping after it is the genuine form of historicism's dominion.

Can we nevertheless portray and represent the dawn of an age in ways different from those of historiography? Perhaps the discipline of

---

Land des Abends, Abend-land. In German *Abendland* means Occident, or "the West," literally "the evening-land."—Tr.

history is still for us an indispensable tool for making the historical contemporary. That does not in any way mean however that historiography, taken by itself, enables us to form within our history a truly adequate, far-reaching relation to history.

The antiquity pervading the Anaximander fragment belongs to the dawn of early times in the land of evening. But what if that which is early outdistanced everything late; if the very earliest far surpassed the very latest? What once occurred in the dawn of our destiny would then come, as what once occurred, at the last (ἔσχατον), that is, at the departure of the long-hidden destiny of Being. The Being of beings is gathered (λέγεσθαι, λόγος) in the ultimacy of its destiny. The essence of Being hitherto disappears, its truth still veiled. The history of Being is gathered in this departure. The gathering in this departure, as the gathering (λόγος) at the outermost point (ἔσχατον) of its essence hitherto, is the eschatology of Being. As something fateful, Being itself is inherently eschatological.

However, in the phrase "eschatology of Being" we do not understand the term "eschatology" as the name of a theological or philosophical discipline. We think of the eschatology of Being in a way corresponding to the way the phenomenology of spirit is to be thought, i.e. from within the history of Being. The phenomenology of spirit itself constitutes a phase in the eschatology of Being, when Being gathers itself in the ultimacy of its essence, hitherto determined through metaphysics, as the absolute subjecticity [Subjektität] of the unconditioned will to will.

If we think within the eschatology of Being, then we must someday anticipate the former dawn in the dawn to come; today we must learn to ponder this former dawn through what is imminent.

If only once we could hear the fragment it would no longer sound like an assertion historically long past. Nor would we be seduced by vain hopes of calculating historically, i.e. philologically and psychologically, what was at one time really present to that man called Anaximander of Miletus which may have served as the condition for his way of representing the world. But presuming we do hear what his saying says, what binds us in our attempt to translate it? How do we get to what is said in the saying, so that it might rescue the translation from arbitrariness?

We are bound to the language of the saying. We are bound to our mother tongue. In both cases we are essentially bound to language and to the experience of its essence. This bond is broader and stronger, but far less apparent, than the standards of all philological and historical facts—which can only borrow their factuality from it. So long as we do not experience this binding, every translation of the fragment must seem wholly arbitrary. Yet even when we are bound to what is said in the saying, not only the translation but also the binding retain the appearance of violence, as though what is to be heard and said here necessarily suffers violence.

Only in thoughtful dialogue with what it says can this fragment of thinking be translated. However, thinking is poetizing, and indeed more than one kind of poetizing, more than poetry and song. Thinking of Being is the original way of poetizing. Language first comes to language, i.e. into its essence, in thinking. Thinking says what the truth of Being dictates; it is the original *dictare*. Thinking is primordial poetry, prior to all poesy, but also prior to the poetics of art, since art shapes its work within the realm of language. All poetizing, in this broader sense, and also in the narrower sense of the poetic, is in its ground a thinking. The poetizing essence of thinking preserves the sway of the truth of Being. Because it poetizes as it thinks, the translation which wishes to let the oldest fragment of thinking itself speak necessarily appears violent.

We shall try to translate the Anaximander fragment. This requires that we translate what is said in Greek into our German tongue. To that end our thinking must first, before translating, be translated to what is said in Greek. Thoughtful translation to what comes to speech in this fragment is a leap over an abyss [*Graben*]. The abyss does not consist merely of the chronological or historical distance of two-and-a-half millennia. It is wider and deeper. It is hard to leap, mainly because we stand right on its edge. We are so near the abyss that we do not have an adequate runway for such a broad jump; we easily fall short—if indeed the lack of a sufficiently solid base allows any leap at all.

What comes to language in the fragment? The question is ambiguous and therefore imprecise. It might mean to inquire into the matter the fragment says something about; it might also mean what the fragment says in itself. More literally translated the fragment says:

But that from which things arise also gives rise to their passing away, according to what is necessary; for things render justice and pay penalty to one another for their injustice, according to the ordinance of time.

According to the usual view the statement speaks of the origin and decay of things. It specifies the nature of this process. Originating and decaying refer back to the place whence they come. Things flower, things fall. Thus they exhibit a kind of barter system in Nature's immutable economy. The exchange of constructive and destructive moments is, of course, only roughly grasped as a general characteristic of natural occurrences. The mutability of all things is therefore not yet represented with precision in terms of motions defined by exact relations of mass. At this point an appropriate formula of the laws of motion is still lacking. The judgment of later, more progressive times is indulgent enough not to ridicule this primitive natural science. Indeed it is found altogether fitting that incipient observation of nature should describe the processes of things in terms of common occurrences in the human sphere. This is why Anaximander's statement mentions justice and injustice, recompense and penalty, sin and retribution, with respect to things. Moral and juridical notions get mixed in with his view of nature. In this regard Theophrastus already criticizes Anaximander for ποιητικωτέροις οὕτως ὀνόμασιν αὐτὰ λέγων, that is, for employing rather poetic words for what he wants to say. Theophrastus means the words δίκη, τίσις, ἀδικία, διδόναι δίκην. . . .

Before all else we should try to make out what the fragment speaks of. Only then can we judge what it says concerning its subject matter.

Considered grammatically, the fragment consists of two clauses. The first begins: ἐξ ὧν δὲ ἡ γένεσίς ἐστι τοῖς οὖσι. . . . The matter under discussion is ὄντα; translated literally, τὰ ὄντα means "beings." The neuter plural appears as τὰ πολλά, "the many," in the sense of the manifold of being. But τὰ ὄντα does not mean an arbitrary or boundless multiplicity; rather, it means τὰ πάντα, the totality of being. Thus τὰ ὄντα means manifold being in totality. The second clause begins: διδόναι γὰρ αὐτά. . . . The αὐτά refers to the τοῖς ὄυσι of the first clause.

The fragment speaks of manifold being in totality. But not only things belong among beings. In the fullest sense, "things" are not only things of nature. Man, things produced by man, and the situation or environment effected and realized by the deeds and omissions of men, also belong among beings, and so do daimonic and divine things. All these are not merely "also" in being; they are even more in being than mere things. The Aristotelian-Theophrastian presupposition that τὰ ὄντα must be φύσει ὄντα, natural things in the narrower sense, is altogether groundless. It is superfluous for our translation. But even the translation of τὰ ὄντα as "the things" does not suit the matter which comes to language in the saying.

If the presupposition that the fragment makes statements about things of nature fails, however, then so does all foundation for the assertion that what ought to be represented strictly in terms of the natural sciences is interpreted morally and juridically. With the collapse of the presupposition that the fragment strives after scientific knowledge concerning the demarcated realm of nature, another assumption becomes superfluous, namely, that at this time ethical or juridical matters were interpreted in terms of the disciplines we call "ethics" and "jurisprudence." Denial of such boundaries between disciplines does not mean to imply that in early times law and ethicality were unknown. But if the way we normally think within a range of disciplines (such as physics, ethics, philosophy of law, biology, psychology) has no place here—if boundaries between these subjects are lacking—then there is no possibility of trespass or of the unjustified transfer of notions from one area to another. Yet where boundaries between disciplines do not appear, boundless indeterminacy and flux do not necessarily prevail: on the contrary, an appropriate articulation of a matter purely thought may well come to language when it has been freed from every oversimplification.

The words δίκη, ἀδικία, and τίσις have a broad significance which cannot be enclosed within the boundaries of particular disciplines. "Broad" does not mean here extensive, in the sense of something flattened or thinned out, but rather far-reaching, rich, containing much thought. For precisely that reason these words are employed: to bring to language the manifold totality in its essential unity. For that to happen, of course, thinking must apprehend the unified totality of the manifold, with its peculiar characteristics, purely in its own terms.

This way of letting manifold being in its unity come into essential view is anything but a kind of primitive and anthropomorphic representation.

In order to translate at all what comes to language in the fragment, we must, before we do any actual translating, consciously cast aside all inadequate presuppositions. For example, that the fragment pertains to the philosophy of nature—in such a way that inappropriate moralisms and legalisms are enmeshed in it; or that highly specialized ideas relevant to particular regions of nature, ethics, or law play a role in it; or finally, that a primitive outlook still prevails which examines the world uncritically, interprets it anthropomorphically, and therefore resorts to poetic expressions.

However, even to cast aside all presuppositions whenever we find them inadequate is insufficient so long as we fail to gain access to what comes to language in the fragment. Dialogue with early Greek thinking will be fruitful only when such listening occurs. It is proper to dialogue that its conversation speak of the same thing; indeed, that it speak out of participation in the Same. According to its wording, the fragment speaks of ὄντα, expressing what they involve and how it is with them. Beings are spoken of in such a way that their Being is expressed. Being comes to language as the Being of beings.

At the summit of the completion of Western philosophy these words are pronounced: "To *stamp* Becoming with the character of Being—that is the *highest will to power*." Thus writes Nietzsche in a note entitled, "Recapitulation." According to the character of the manuscript's handwriting we must locate it in the year 1885, about the time when Nietzsche, having completed *Zarathustra*, was planning his systematic metaphysical *magnum opus*. The "Being" Nietzsche thinks here is "the eternal recurrence of the same." It is the way of continuance through which will to power wills itself and guarantees its own presencing as the Being of Becoming. At the outermost point of the completion of metaphysics the Being of beings is addressed in these words.

The ancient fragment of early Western thinking and the late fragment of recent Western thinking bring the Same to language, but what they say is not identical. However, where we can speak of the Same in terms of things which are not identical, the fundamental condition of a thoughtful dialogue between recent and early times is automatically fulfilled.

Or does it only seem so? Does there lie behind this "seeming" a gap between the language of our thinking and the language of Greek philosophy? Whatever the case, if we take τὰ ὄντα to mean "beings" and εἶναι as nothing else than "to be," we cross every gap; granting the differences between these epochs, we are together with the early thinkers in the realm of the Same. This Same secures our translation of τὰ ὄντα and εἶναι by "beings" and "to be." Must we place in evidence extensive texts of Greek philosophy in order to demonstrate the unimpeachable correctness of this translation? All interpretations of Greek philosophy themselves already rest on this translation. Every lexicon provides the most copious information concerning these words, εἶναι meaning "to be," ἔστιν "is," ὄν "being," and τὰ ὄντα "beings."

So it is in fact. We do not mean to express doubts about it. We do not ask whether ὄν is correctly translated as "being" and εἶναι as "to be"; we ask only whether in this correct translation we also think correctly. We ask only whether in this most common of all translations anything at all is thought.

Let us see. Let us examine ourselves and others. It becomes manifest that in this correct translation everything is embroiled in equivocal and imprecise significations. It becomes clear that the always hasty approximations of usual translations are never seen as insufficient; nor are scholarly research and writing ever disturbed by them. Perhaps great effort is expended in order to bring out what the Greeks truly represented to themselves in words like θεός, ψυχή, ζωή, τύχη, χάρις, λόγος, φύσις, or words like ἰδέα, τέχνη, and ἐνέργεια. But we do not realize that these and similar labors get nowhere and come to nothing so long as they do not satisfactorily clarify that realm of all realms—so long as they do not cast sufficient light on ὄν and εἶναι in their Greek essence. But scarcely have we named εἶναι as a realm than "realm" is represented by the logical apparatus of γένος and κοινόν, and understood in the sense of the universal and all-encompassing. This grasping together *(concipere)* in the manner of representational concepts is immediately taken to be the only possible way to understand Being. It is still taken to be applicable when one hastens into the dialectic of concepts or flees to a nonconceptual realm of mystic signs. It is wholly forgotten that the potency of the concept and the interpretation of thinking as conceiving rest solely on the unthought, because unexperienced, essence of ὄν and εἶναι.

Most often we thoughtlessly catalogue the words ὄν and εἶναι under what we mean by the corresponding (but unthought) words of our own mother tongue, "being" and "to be." More precisely, we never ascribe a significance to the Greek words at all: we immediately adopt them from our stock of common knowledge, which has already endowed them with the common intelligibility of its own language. We support the Greek words with nothing except the complacent negligence of hasty opinion. This may do in a pinch, when for example we are reading εἶναι and ἔστιν in Thucydides' historical works, or ἦν and ἔσται in Sophocles.

But what if τὰ ὄντα, ὄν, and εἶναι come to speak in language as the fundamental words of thinking, and not simply a particular kind of thinking but rather as the key words for all Western thinking? Then an examination of the language employed in the translation would reveal the following state of affairs:

Neither is it clear and firmly established what we ourselves are thinking in the words "being" and "to be" in our own language;

nor is it clear and firmly established whether anything we are liable to come up with suits what the Greeks were addressing in the words ὄν and εἶναι.

Neither is it at all clear and firmly established what ὄν and εἶναι, thought in Greek, say;

nor can we, granted this state of affairs, administer an examination which might determine whether and how far our thinking corresponds to that of the Greeks.

These simple relations remain thoroughly confused and unthought. But within them, hovering over them, Being-talk has drifted far and wide, all at sea. Buoyed by the formal correctness of the translation of ὄν and εἶναι by "being" and "to be," drifting right on by the confused state of affairs, Being-talk deceives. But not only do we contemporary men err in this confusion; all the notions and representations we have inherited from Greek philosophy remain in the same confusion, exiled for millennia. Neither pure neglect on the part of philology nor inadequate historical research has occasioned this confusion. It arises from the abyss [*Abgrund*] of that relation by which Being has appropriated the essence of Western man. We cannot therefore dissolve the confusion by elaborating through some definition a more precise meaning for the words ὄν and εἶναι, "being" and "to be." On the contrary, the attempt to heed this confusion steadfastly, using its tenacious power to effect some resolution, may well bring about a situation which releases a different destiny of Being. The preparation of such an occasion is already sufficient reason to set in motion, within the abiding confusion, a conversation with early thinking.

If we so stubbornly insist on thinking Greek thought in Greek fashion it is by no means because we intend to sketch a historical portrait of Greek antiquity, as one of the past great ages of man, which would be in many respects more accurate. We search for what is Greek neither for the sake of the Greeks themselves nor for the advancement of scholarship. Nor do we desire a more meaningful conversation simply for its own sake. Rather, our sole aim is to reach what wants to come to language in such a conversation, provided it come of its own accord. And this is that Same which fatefully concerns the Greeks and ourselves, albeit in different ways. It is that which brings the dawn of thinking into the fate of things Western, into the land of evening. Only as a result of this fatefulness [*Geschick*] do the Greeks become Greeks in the historic [*geschichtlich*] sense.

In our manner of speaking, "Greek" does not designate a particular people or nation, nor a cultural or anthropological group. What is Greek is the dawn of that destiny in which Being illuminates itself in beings and so propounds a certain essence of man; that essence unfolds historically as something fateful, preserved in Being and dispensed by Being, without ever being separated from Being.

Greek antiquity, Christendom, modern times, global affairs, and the West interpreted as the land of evening—we are thinking all these on the basis of a fundamental characteristic of Being which is more concealed in Λήθη than it is revealed in 'Αλήθεια. Yet this concealing of its essence and of its essential origin is characteristic of Being's primordial self-illumination, so much so that thinking simply does *not* pursue it. The being itself does not step into this light of Being. The unconcealment of beings, the brightness granted them, obscures the light of Being.

As it reveals itself in beings, Being withdraws.

In this way, by illuminating them, Being sets beings adrift in errancy. Beings come to pass in that errancy by which they circumvent Being and establish the realm of error (in the sense of a prince's realm or the realm of poetry). Error is the space in which history unfolds. In error what happens in history bypasses what is like Being. Therefore, whatever unfolds historically is necessarily misinterpreted. During the course of this misinterpretation destiny awaits what will become of its seed. It brings those whom it concerns to the possibilities of the fateful and fatal [*Geschicklichen und Ungeschicklichen*]. Man's destiny gropes toward its fate [*Geschick versucht sich an Geschick*]. Man's inability to see himself corresponds to the self-concealing of the lighting of Being.

Without errancy there would be no connection from destiny to destiny: there would be no history. Chronological distance and causal sequence do indeed belong to the discipline of historiography, but are not themselves history. When we are historical we are neither a great nor a small distance from what is Greek. Rather, we are in errancy toward it.

As it reveals itself in beings, Being withdraws.

Being thereby holds to its truth and keeps to itself. This keeping to itself is the way it reveals itself early on. Its early sign is 'Α–λήθεια. As it provides the unconcealment of beings it founds the concealment of Being. Concealment remains characteristic of that denial by which it keeps to itself.

We may call this luminous keeping to itself in the truth of its essence the έποχή of Being. However, this word, borrowed from the Stoic philosophers, does not here have the Husserlian sense of object-ification or methodical exclusion by an act of thetic consciousness. The *epoche* of Being belongs to Being itself; we are thinking it in terms of the experience of the oblivion of Being.

From the *epoche* of Being comes the epochal essence of its destining, in which world history properly consists. When Being keeps to itself in its destining, world suddenly and unexpectedly comes to pass. Every epoch of world history is an epoch of errancy. The epochal nature of Being belongs to the concealed temporal character of Being and designates the essence of time as thought in Being. What is represented in this word "time" is only the vacuity of an illusory time derived from beings conceived as objects.

For us, however, the most readily experienced correspondence to the epochal character of Being is the ecstatic character of *Da-sein*. The epochal essence of Being lays claim to the ecstatic nature of *Da-sein*. The *ek-sistence* of man sustains what is ecstatic and so preserves what is epochal in Being, to whose essence the *Da*, and thereby *Da-sein*, belongs.

The beginning of the epoch of Being lies in that which we call "Greek," thought epochally. This beginning, also to be thought epochally, is the dawn of the destiny in Being from Being.

Little depends on what we represent and portray of the past; but much depends on the way we are mindful of what is destined. Can we ever be mindful without thinking? But if thinking does occur we abandon all claims of shortsighted opinion and open ourselves to the claim of destiny. Does this claim speak in the early saying of Anaximander?

We are not sure whether its claim speaks to our essential being. It remains to ask whether in our relation to the truth of Being the glance of Being, and this means lightning (Heraclitus, fr. 64), strikes; or whether in our knowledge of the past only the faintest glimmers of a storm long flown cast a pale semblance of light.

Does the fragment speak to us of ὄντα in their Being? Do we apprehend what it says, the εἶναι of beings? Does a streak of light still pierce the misty confusion of errancy and tell us what ὄντα and εἶναι say in Greek? Only in the brilliance of this lightning streak can we translate ourselves to what is said in the fragment, so as to translate it in thoughtful conversation. Perhaps the confusion surrounding the use of the words ὄντα and εἶναι, "being" and "to be," comes less from the fact that language cannot say everything adequately than because we cannot think through the matter involved clearly enough. Lessing once said, "Language can express everything we can clearly think." So it rests with us to be ready for the right opportunity, which will permit us to think clearly the matter the fragment brings to language.

We are inclined to see the opportunity we are looking for in the Anaximander fragment itself. In that case we still are not paying sufficient heed to what the way of translating requires.

For before interpreting the fragment—and not with its help to begin with—it is essential that we translate ourselves to the source of what comes to language in it, which is to say, to τὰ ὄντα. This word indicates the source from which the fragment speaks, not merely that which it expresses. That from which it speaks is already, before any expression, what is spoken by the Greek language in common everyday parlance as well as in its learned employ. We must therefore seek the opportunity which will let us cross over to that source first of all outside the fragment itself; it must be an opportunity which will let us experience what τὰ ὄντα, thought in Greek, says. Furthermore, we must at first remain outside the fragment because we have not yet delineated each of its terms; this delineation is ultimately (or, in terms of the matter itself, in the first place) governed by the knowledge of what in early times was thought or thinkable in such a choice of words, as distinct from what the prevailing notions of recent times find in it.

The text cited and translated above from Simplicius' commentary on the *Physics* is traditionally accepted as the Anaximander fragment. However, the commentary does not cite the fragment so clearly that we can ascertain with certainty where Anaximander's saying begins and where it ends. Still, our contemporaries who are exceptionally knowledgeable in the Greek language accept the text of the fragment in the form introduced at the outset of our inquiry.

But even John Burnet, the distinguished scholar of Greek philosophy to whom we owe the Oxford edition of Plato, in his book *Early Greek Philosophy* expressed doubts as to whether Simplicius' citation begins where it is usually said to begin. In opposition to Diels, Burnet writes: "Diels (*Vors.* 2, 9) begins the actual quotation with the words ἐξ ὧν δὲ ἡ γένεσις. . . . The Greek practice of blending quotations with the text tells against this. [Only seldom does a Greek author immediately begin with a literal quotation.] Further it is safer not to ascribe the terms γένεσις and φθορά in their technical Platonic sense to Anaximander [and it is not likely that Anaximander said anything about τὰ ὄντα]."*

On this basis Burnet argues that Anaximander's saying begins only with the words κατὰ τὸ χρεών. What Burnet says in general about Greek citations speaks for the exclusion of the words preceding these. On the other hand his remarks, which rest on the terminological employment of the words γένεσις and φθορά, cannot be accepted as they stand. It is correct to say that γένεσις and φθορά become conceptual terms with Plato and Aristotle and their schools. But γένεσις and φθορά are old words which even Homer knows. Anaximander need not have employed them as conceptual terms. He cannot have applied them in this fashion, because conceptual language necessarily remains foreign to him. For conceptual language is first possible on the basis of the interpretation of Being as ἰδέα, and indeed from then on it is unavoidable.

Nevertheless, the entire sentence preceding the κατὰ τὸ χρεών is much more Aristotelian in structure and tone than archaic. The κατὰ τὴν τοῦ χρόνου τάξιν at the end of the normally accepted text also betrays the same characteristic lateness. Whoever takes it upon himself to strike out the part of the text which is dubious to Burnet cannot maintain the usually accepted closing of the fragment either. Of Anaximander's original words, only these would remain:

κατὰ τὸ χρεών· διδόναι γὰρ αὐτὰ δίκην καὶ τίσιν ἀλλήλοις τῆς ἀδικίας.

. . . according to necessity; for they pay one another recompense and penalty for their injustice.

*Heidegger cites the German translation of Burnet's third edition by Else Schenkl, *Die Anfänge der griechischen Philosophie* (Berlin: Teubner, 1913), p. 43, n. 4. I have cited the fourth English edition (London: Black, 1930), p. 52, n. 6, said to be "a reprint of the third edition" with "additional references and one correction." The first bracketed phrase does not occur in the English but appears in Schenkl's translation; the second does occur in the English but not in the German. Nevertheless, the first is a natural expansion of Burnet's view; as for the second, one might expect that Heidegger's response to Burnet regarding τὰ ὄντα would duplicate that respecting γένεσις and φθορά: although not yet a technical term, τὰ ὄντα is an old word, known already by Homer in the form τ' ἐόντα, as the *Iliad* passage below (p. 33) attests.—TR.

Now these are precisely the words in reference to which Theophrastus complains that Anaximander speaks in a rather poetic manner. Since thinking through this entire question, which came up often in my lecture courses a few years ago, I am inclined to accept only these as the immediate, genuine words of Anaximander, with the proviso however that the preceding parts of the text are not simply set aside, but rather are positively retained, on the basis of the strength and eloquence of their thought, as secondary testimony concerning Anaximander's thinking. This demands that we understand precisely these words γένεσις and φθορά as they are thought in Greek, whether they be preconceptual words or Platonic-Aristotelian conceptual terms.

Accordingly, γένεσις does not at all mean the genetic in the sense of the "developmental" as conceived in modern times; nor does φθορά mean the counterphenomenon to development—some sort of regression, shrinkage, or wasting away. Rather, γένεσις and φθορά are to be thought from φύσις, and within it, as ways of luminous rising and decline. Certainly we can translate γένεσις as origination; but we must think this originating as a movement which lets every emerging being abandon concealment and go forward into unconcealment. Certainly we can translate φθορά as passing away; but we must think this passing away as a going which in its turn abandons unconcealment, departing and withdrawing into concealment.

Presumably, Anaximander spoke of γένεσις and φθορά. It remains questionable whether this occurred in the form of the traditional statement, although such paradoxical turns of speech as γένεσις ἔστιν (which is the way I should like to read it) and φθορά γίνεται, "coming-to-be *is*," and "passing-away comes to be" still may speak in favor of an ancient language. Γένεσις is coming forward and arriving in unconcealment. Φθορά means the departure and descent into concealment of what has arrived there out of unconcealment. The coming forward into . . . and the departure to . . . *become present* within unconcealment between what is concealed and what is unconcealed. They initiate the arrival and departure of whatever has arrived.

Anaximander must have spoken of what is designated in γένεσις and φθορά: whether he actually mentioned τὰ ὄντα remains an open question, although nothing speaks against it. The αὐτά in the second clause, because of the scope of what it says and also because of the reference of this second clause back to the κατὰ τὸ χρεών, can designate nothing less than being-in-totality experienced in a preconceptual way, τὰ πολλά, τὰ πάντα, "beings." We are still calling τὰ ὄντα "beings" without ever having clarified what ὄν and εἶναι indicate when thought in Greek. Yet we have in the meantime won a more open field in which to pursue such clarification.

We began with the usually accepted text of the fragment. In a preliminary review of it we excluded the common presuppositions which determine its interpretation. In so doing we discovered a clue in what comes to language in γένεσις and φθορά. The fragment speaks of that which, as it approaches, arrives in unconcealment, and which, having arrived here, departs by withdrawing into the distance.

However, whatever has its essence in such arrival and departure we would like to call becoming and perishing, which is to say, transiency rather than being; because we have for a long time been accustomed to set Being opposite Becoming, as if Becoming were a kind of nothingness and did not even belong to Being; and this because Being has for a long time been understood to be nothing else than sheer perdurance. Nevertheless, if Becoming *is*, then we must think Being so essentially that it does not simply include Becoming in some vacuous conceptual manner, but rather in such a way that Being sustains and characterizes Becoming (γένεσις-φθορά) in an essential, appropriate manner.

In this regard we are not to discuss whether and with what right we should represent Becoming as transiency. Rather, we must discuss what sort of essence the Greeks think for Being when in the realm of the ὄντα they experience approach and withdrawal as the basic trait of advent.

When the Greeks say τὰ ὄντα, what comes to the fore in their language? Where is there, aside from the Anaximander fragment, a guideline which would translate us there? Because the word in question, with all its modifications, ἔστιν, ἦν, ἔσται, εἶναι, speaks everywhere throughout the language—and even before thinking actually chooses this as its fundamental word—it is necessary that we avail ourselves of an opportunity which in terms of its subject matter, its time, and the realm to which it belongs, lies outside philosophy, and which from every point of view precedes the pronouncements of thinking.

In Homer we perceive such an opportunity. Thanks to him we possess a reference in which the word appears as something more than a term in the lexicon. Rather, it is a reference which poetically brings to language what ὄντα names. Because all λέξις of the lexicographic sort presupposes the thought of the λεγόμενον, we will refrain from the futile practice of heaping up references to serve as evidence; this kind of annotation usually proves only that none of the references has been thought through. With the aid of this commonly adopted method one usually expects that by shoving together one unclarified reference with another every bit as unclear clarity will suddenly result.

The passage upon which we wish to comment is found at the beginning of the first book of the *Iliad*, lines 68-72. It gives us the chance to cross over to what the Greeks designate with the word ὄντα, provided we let ourselves be transported by the poet to the distant shore of the matter spoken there.

For the following reference a preliminary observation concerning the history of the language is needed. Our observations cannot claim to present this philological problem adequately, much less to solve it. In Plato and Aristotle we encounter the words ὄν and ὄντα as conceptual terms. The later terms "ontic" and "ontological" are formed from them. However, ὄν and ὄντα, considered linguistically, are presumably somewhat truncated forms of the original words ἐόν and ἐόντα. Only in the latter words is the sound preserved which relates them to ἔστιν and εἶναι. The epsilon in ἐόν and ἐόντα is the epsilon in the root ἐσ of ἔστιν, *est, esse,* and "is." In contrast ὄν and ὄντα appear as rootless participial endings, as though by themselves they expressly designated what we must think in those word-forms called by later grammarians μετοχή, *participium,* i.e. those word-forms which participate in the verbal and nominal senses of a word.

Thus ὄν says "being" in the sense of *to be* a being; at the same time it names a *being* which is. In the duality of the participial significance of ὄν the distinction between "to be" and "a being" lies concealed. What is here set forth, which at first may be taken for grammatical hair-splitting, is in truth the riddle of Being. The participle ὄν is the word for what comes to appear in metaphysics as transcendental and transcendent Transcendence.

Archaic language, and thus Parmenides and Heraclitus as well, always employ ἐόν and ἐόντα.

But ἐόν, "being," is not only the singular form of the participle ἐόντα, "beings"; rather, it indicates what is singular as such, what is singular in its numerical unity and what is singularly and unifyingly one before all number.

We might assert in an exaggerated way, which nevertheless bears on the truth, that the fate of the West hangs on the translation of the word ἐόν, assuming that the translation consists in *crossing over* to the truth of what comes to language in ἐόν.

What does Homer tell us about this word? We are familiar with the situation of the Achaeans before Troy at the outset of the *Iliad.* For nine days the plague sent by Apollo has raged in the Greek camp. At an assembly of the warriors Achilles commands Kalchas the seer to interpret the wrath of the god.

> . . . τοῖσι δ' ἀνέστη
> Κάλχας Θεστορίδης οἰωνοπόλων ὄχ' ἄριστος
> ὅς ἤδη τά τ' ἐόντα τά τ' ἐσσόμενα πρό τ' ἐόντα
> καὶ νήεσσ' ἡγήσατ' Ἀχαιῶν Ἴλιον εἴσω
> ἥν διὰ μαντοσύνην, τήν οἱ πόρε Φοῖβος Ἀπόλλων·

> . . . and among them stood up
> Kalchas, Thestor's son, far the best of the bird interpreters,
> who knew all that is, is to be, or once was,
> who guided into the land of Ilion the ships of the Achaeans
> through that seercraft of his own that Phoibos Apollo gave him.*

Before he lets Kalchas speak, Homer designates him as the seer. Whoever belongs in the realm of seers is such a one ὅς ἤδη . . . "who knew . . ."; ἤδη is the pluperfect of the perfect οἶδεν, "he has seen."

---

*Homer, *The Iliad,* trans. Richmond Lattimore (Chicago: University of Chicago Press, 1961), p. 61, with minor changes. Heidegger uses the German translation by Voss.—Tr.

Only when a man has seen does he truly see. To see is to have seen. What is seen has arrived and remains for him in sight. A seer has always already seen. Having seen in advance he sees into the future. He sees the future tense out of the perfect. When the poet speaks of the seer's seeing as a having-seen, he must say what the seer has seen in the pluperfect tense, ἤδη, he had seen. What is it that the seer has seen in advance? Obviously, only what becomes present in the lighting that penetrates his sight. What is seen in such a seeing can only be what comes to presence in unconcealment. But what becomes present? The poet names something threefold; τά τ'ἐόντα, that which is in being, τά τ̓ ἐσσόμενα, also that which will be, πρό τ̓ ἐοντα, and also the being that once was.

The first point we gather from this poetic phrase is that τὰ ἐόντα is distinguished from τὰ ἐσσόμενα and πρὸ ἐόντα. Thus τὰ ἐόντα designates being in the sense of the present [*Gegenwärtigen*]. When we moderns speak of "the present," we either mean what is "now"—which we represent as something within time, the "now" serving as a phase in the stream of time—or we bring the "present" into relation with the "objective" [*Gegenständigen*]. As something objective, an object is related to a representing subject. However, if we employ "present" for the sake of a closer determination of ἐόντα, then we must understand "the present" from the essence of ἐόντα and not vice versa. Yet ἐόντα is also what is past and what is to come. Both are ways of presencing, i.e. the presencing of what is not presently present. The Greeks also named more precisely what is presently present τὰ παρεόντα, παρά meaning "alongside," in the sense of coming alongside in unconcealment. The *gegen* in *gegenwärtig* [presently] does not mean something over against a subject, but rather an open expanse [*Gegend*] of unconcealment, into which and within which whatever comes along lingers. Accordingly, as a characteristic of ἐόντα, "presently" means as much as "having arrived to linger awhile in the expanse of unconcealment." Spoken first, and thus emphasized, ἐόντα, which is expressly distinguished from προεόντα and ἐσσόμενα, names for the Greeks what is present insofar as it has arrived in the designated sense, to linger within the expanse of unconcealment. Such a coming is proper arrival, the presencing of what is properly present. What is past and what is to come also become present, namely as outside the expanse of unconcealment. What presents itself as non-present is what is absent. As such it remains essentially related to what is presently present, inasmuch as it either comes forward into the expanse of unconcealment or withdraws from it. Even what is absent is something present, for *as* absent from the expanse, it presents itself in unconcealment. What is past and what is to come are also ἐόντα. Consequently ἐόν means becoming present in unconcealment.

The conclusion of this commentary on ἐόντα is that also in Greek experience what comes to presence remains ambiguous, and indeed necessarily so. On the one hand, τὰ ἐόντα means what is presently present; on the other, it also means all that becomes present, whether at the present time or not. However, we must never represent what is present in the broader sense as the "universal concept" of presence as opposed to a particular case—the presently present—though this is what the usual conceptual mode of thought suggests. For in fact it is precisely the presently present and the unconcealment that rules in it that pervade the essence of what is absent, as that which is not presently present.

The seer stands in sight of what is present, in its unconcealment, which has at the same time cast light on the concealment of what is absent as being absent. The seer sees inasmuch as he has seen everything as present; καί, and only on that account, νῄεσσ' ἡγήσατ', was he able to lead the Achaeans' ships to Troy. He was able to do this through God-given μαντοσύνη. The seer, ὁ μάντις, is the μαινόμενος, the madman. But in what does the essence of madness consist? A madman is beside himself, outside himself: he is away. We ask: away? Where to and where from? Away from the sheer oppression of what lies before us, which is only presently present, away to what is absent; and at the same time away to what is presently present insofar as this is always only something that arrives in the course of its coming and going. The seer is outside himself in the solitary region of the presencing of everything that in some way becomes present. Therefore he can find his way back from the "away" of this region, and arrive at what has just presented itself, namely, the raging epidemic. The madness of the seer's being away does not require that he rave, roll his eyes, and toss his limbs; the simple tranquility of bodily composure may accompany the madness of vision.

All things present and absent are gathered and preserved in *one* presencing for the seer. The old German word *war* [was] means protection. We still recognize this in *wahrnehmen* [to perceive], i.e. to take into preservation; in *gewahren* and *verwahren* [to be aware of, to keep or preserve]. We must think of *wahren* as a securing which clears and gathers. Presencing preserves [*wahrt*] in unconcealment what is present both at the present time and not at the present time. The seer speaks from the preserve [*Wahr*] of what is present. He is the soothsayer [*Wahr-Sager*].

Here we think of the preserve in the sense of that gathering which clears and shelters; it suggests itself as a long-hidden fundamental trait of presencing, i.e. of Being. One day we shall learn to think our exhausted word for truth [*Wahrheit*] in terms of the preserve; to experience truth as the preservation [*Wahrnis*] of Being; and to understand that, as presencing, Being belongs to this preservation. As protection of Being, preservation belongs to the herdsman, who has so little to do with bucolic idylls and Nature mysticism that he can be the herdsman of Being only if he continues to hold the place of nothingness. Both are the Same. Man can do both only within the openedness of *Da-sein*.

The seer is the one who has already seen the totality of what is present in its presencing. Said in Latin, *vidit;* in German, *er steht im Wissen* [he stands in knowledge]. To have seen is the essence of knowing. In "to have seen" there is always something more at play than the completion of an optical process. In it the connection with what is present subsists behind every kind of sensuous or nonsensuous grasping. On that account, "to have seen" is related to self-illuminating presencing. Seeing is determined, not by the eye, but by the lighting of Being. Presence within the lighting articulates all the human senses. The essence of seeing, as "to have seen," is to know. Knowledge embraces vision and remains indebted to presencing. Knowledge is remembrance of Being. That is why Μνημοσύνη is mother of the muses. Knowledge is not science in the modern sense. Knowledge is thoughtful maintenance of Being's preserve.

Whither have Homer's words translated us? Τὸ ἐόντα. The

Greeks experience beings as being present, whether at the present time or not, presencing in unconcealment. The word by which we translate ὄν, "being," is now no longer obtuse; no longer are "to be," as the translation of εἶναι, and the Greek word itself hastily employed ciphers for arbitrary and vague notions about some indeterminate universal.

At the same time it becomes manifest that Being, as the presencing of what is present, is already in itself truth, provided we think the essence of truth as the gathering that clears and shelters; provided we dissociate ourselves from the modern prejudice of metaphysics—today accepted as something obvious—that truth is a property of beings or of Being. Being, saying the word thoughtfully now, is εἶναι as presencing. In a hidden way it is a property of truth, but clearly not of truth considered as a characteristic of human or divine cognition, and not as a property in the sense of a quality. Furthermore, it has become clear that τὰ ἐόντα ambiguously names what is presently present and also what is not presently present; the latter, understood with regard to the former, means what is absent. But what is at the present time present is not a slice of something sandwiched between two absences. If what is present stands in the forefront of vision, everything presences together: one brings the other with it, one lets the other go. What is presently present in unconcealment lingers in unconcealment as in an open expanse. Whatever lingers (or whiles) in the expanse proceeds to it from concealment and arrives in unconcealment. But what is present *is* arriving or lingering insofar as it is also already departing from unconcealment toward concealment. What is presently present lingers awhile. It endures in approach and withdrawal. Lingering is the transition from coming to going: what is present is what in each case lingers. Lingering in transition, it lingers still in approach and lingers already in departure. What is for the time being present, what presently is, comes to presence out of absence. This must be said precisely of whatever is truly present, although our usual way of representing things would like to exclude from what is present all absence.

Τὰ ἐόντα names the unique manifold of whatever lingers awhile. Everything present in unconcealment in this way presents itself to all others, each after its own fashion.

Finally, we gather something else from the passage in Homer: τὰ ἐόντα, so-called beings, does not mean exclusively the things of nature. In the present instance the poet applies ἐόντα to the Achaeans' encampment before Troy, the god's wrath, the plague's fury, funeral pyres, the perplexity of the leaders, and so on. In Homer's language τὰ ἐόντα is not a conceptual philosophical term but a thoughtful and thoughtfully uttered word. It does not specify natural things, nor does it at all indicate objects which stand over against human representation. Man too belongs to ἐόντα; he is that present being which, illuminating, apprehending, and thus gathering, lets what is present as such become present in unconcealment. If in the poetic designation of Kalchas what is present is thought in relation to the seer's seeing, this means for Greek thinking that the seer, as the one who has seen, is himself one who makes-present and belongs in an exceptional sense to the totality of what is present. On the other hand, it does not mean that what is present is nothing but an object wholly dependent upon the seer's subjectivity.

Τὰ ἐόντα, what is present, whether or not at the present time, is the unobtrusive name of what expressly comes to language in the Anaximander fragment. This word names that which, while not yet spoken, is the unspoken in thinking which addresses all thinking. This word names that which from now on, whether or not it is uttered, lays a claim on all Western thinking.

But only several decades later, not with Anaximander but with Parmenides, ἐόν (presencing) and εἶναι (to presence) are expressed as the fundamental words of Western thinking. This does not happen, as the normal misconception still insists, because Parmenides interprets being "logically" in terms of a proposition's structure and its copula. In the history of Greek thinking even Aristotle did not go so far when he thought the Being of beings in terms of κατηγορία. Aristotle perceived beings as what already lies before any proposition, which is to say, as what is present and lingers awhile in unconcealment. Aristotle did not have to interpret substance, ὑποκείμενον, on the basis of the subject of a predicate phrase, because the essence of substance, οὐσία, in the sense of παρουσία, was already granted. Nor did Aristotle think the presence of what is present in terms of the objectivity of an object in a proposition, but rather as ἐνέργεια, which however is far removed—as by an abyss—from the *actualitas* of *actus purus* in medieval scholasticism.

In any case, Parmenides' ἔστιν does not mean the "is" which is the copula of a proposition. It names ἐόν, the presencing of what is present. The ἔστιν corresponds to the pure claim of Being, before the division into a first and second οὐσία, into *existentia* and *essentia*. But in this way, ἐόν is thought from the concealed and undisclosed richness of unconcealment in ἐόντα known to the early Greeks, without it ever becoming possible or necessary for them to experience in all its perspectives this essential richness itself.

From a thoughtful experience of the ἐόν of ἐόντα, spoken in a preconceptual way, the fundamental words for early thinking are uttered: Φύσις and Λόγος, Μοῖρα and Ἔρις, Ἀλήθεια and Ἕν. By means of the Ἕν, which is to be thought back into the realm of fundamental words, ἐόν and εἶναι become the words which expressly indicate what is present. Only as a result of the destiny of Being, as the destiny of Ἕν, does the modern age after essential upheavals enter the epoch of the monadology of substance, which completes itself in the phenomenology of spirit.

It is not that Parmenides interpreted Being logically. On the contrary, having sprung from metaphysics, which at the same time it wholly dominated, logic led to a state of affairs where the essential richness of Being hidden in these early fundamental words remained buried. Thus Being could be driven to the fatal extreme of serving as the emptiest, most universal concept.

But since the dawn of thinking "Being" names the presencing of what is present, in the sense of the gathering which clears and shelters, which in turn is thought and designated as the Λόγος. The Λόγος (λέγειν, to gather or assemble) is experienced through Ἀλήθεια, the sheltering which reveals things. In the bifurcated essense of Ἀλήθεια, what is essentially thought as Ἔρις and Μοῖρα, which at the same time mean Φύσις, lies concealed.

In the language of these fundamental words, thought from the experience of presencing, these words from the Anaximander fragment resound: δίκη, τίσις, ἀδικία.

The claim of Being which speaks in these words determines

philosophy in its essence. Philosophy did not spring from myth. It arises solely from thinking and in thinking. But thinking is the thinking of Being. Thinking does not originate: it is, when Being presences. But the collapse of thinking into the sciences and into faith is the baneful destiny of Being.

In the dawn of Being's destiny, beings, τὰ ἐόντα, come to language. From the restrained abundance of what in this way comes, what does the Anaximander fragment bring to utterance? According to the presumably genuine text, the fragment reads:

. . . κατὰ τὸ χρεών· διδόναι γὰρ αὐτὰ δίκην καὶ τίσιν ἀλλήλοις τῆς ἀδικίας.

In the standard translation:

. . . according to necessity; for they pay one another recompense and penalty for their injustice.

The fragment still consists of two clauses; of the first one only the closing words are retained. We will begin by commenting on the second clause.

The αὐτά refers to what is named in the previous clause. The antecedent can only be τὰ ὄντα, the totality of what is present, whatever is present in unconcealment, whether or not at the present time. Whether or not this is expressly designated by the word ἐόντα may remain an open question since the text is uncertain. The αὐτά refers to everything present, everything that presences by lingering awhile: gods and men, temples and cities, sea and land, eagle and snake, tree and shrub, wind and light, stone and sand, day and night. What is present coheres in unifying presencing, as everything becomes present to everything else within its duration; it becomes present and lingers with the others. This multiplicity (πολλά) is not a muster of separate objects behind which something stands, embracing them as a whole. Rather, presencing as such is ruled by the lingering-with-one-another of a concealed gathering. Thus Heraclitus, catching sight of this essential gathering, unifying, and revealing in presencing, named the Ἕν (the Being of beings) the Λόγος.

But before this, how does Anaximander experience the totality of things present; how does he experience their having arrived to linger awhile among one another in unconcealment? What at bottom runs through whatever is present? The fragment's last word gives the answer. We must begin the translation with it. This word designates the basic trait of what is present: ἡ ἀδικία. The literal translation is "injustice." But is this literal translation faithful? That is to say: does the word which translates ἀδικία heed what comes to language in the saying? Does the αὐτά, the totality of what is present, lingering awhile in unconcealment, stand before our eyes?

How is what lingers awhile in presence unjust? What is unjust about it? Is it not the right of whatever is present that in each case it linger awhile, endure, and so fulfill its presencing?

The word ἀ–δικία immediately suggests that δίκη is absent. We are accustomed to translate δίκη as "right." The translations even use "penalties" to translate "right." If we resist our own juridical-moral notions, if we restrict ourselves to what comes to language, then we hear that wherever ἀδικία rules all is not right with things. That means, something is out of joint. But of what are we speaking? Of what is present, lingering awhile. But where are there jointures in what is present? Or where is there even one jointure? How can what is present without jointure be ἄδικον, out of joint?

The fragment clearly says that what is present is in ἀδικία, i.e. is out of joint. However, that cannot mean that things no longer come to presence. But neither does it say that what is present is only occasionally, or perhaps only with respect to some one of its properties, out of joint. The fragment says: what is present as such, being what it is, is out of joint. To presencing as such jointure must belong, thus creating the possibility of its being out of joint. What is present is that which lingers awhile. The while occurs essentially as the transitional arrival in departure: the while comes to presence between approach and withdrawal. Between this twofold absence the presencing of all that lingers occurs. In this "between" whatever lingers awhile is joined. This "between" is the jointure in accordance with which whatever lingers is joined, from its emergence here to its departure away from here. The presencing of whatever lingers obtrudes into the "here" of its coming, as into the "away" of its going. In both directions presencing is conjointly disposed toward absence. Presencing comes about in such a jointure. What is present emerges by approaching and passes away by departing; it does both at the same time, indeed because it lingers. The "while" occurs essentially in the jointure.

But then what lingers awhile is precisely in the jointure of its presencing, and not at all, as we might put it, in disjunction, ἀδικία. But the fragment says it is. The fragment speaks from the essential experience that ἀδικία is the fundamental trait of ἐόντα.

Whatever lingers awhile becomes present as it lingers in the jointure which arranges presencing jointly between a twofold absence. Still, as what is present, whatever lingers awhile—and only it—can stay the length of its while. What has arrived may even insist upon its while solely to remain more present, in the sense of perduring. That which lingers perseveres in its presencing. In this way it extricates itself from its transitory while. It strikes the willful pose of persistence, no longer concerning itself with whatever else is present. It stiffens—as if this were the way to linger—and aims solely for continuance and subsistence.

Coming to presence in the jointure of the while, what is present abandons that jointure and is, in terms of whatever lingers awhile, in disjunction. Everything that lingers awhile stands in disjunction. To the presencing of what is present, to the ἐόν of ἐόντα, ἀδικία belongs. Thus, standing in disjunction would be the essence of all that is present. And so in this early fragment of thinking the pessimism—not to say the nihilism—of the Greek experience of Being would come to the fore.

However, does the fragment say that the essence of what is present consists in disjunction? It does and it doesn't. Certainly, the fragment designates disjunction as the fundamental trait of what is present, but only to say:

διδόναι γὰρ αὐτὰ δίκην . . . τῆς ἀδικίας.

"They must pay penalty," Nietzsche translates; "They pay recompense," Diels translates, "for their injustice." But the fragment says nothing about payment, recompense, and penalty; nor does it say that something is punishable, or even must be avenged, according to the opinion of those who equate justice with vengeance.

Meanwhile, the thoughtlessly uttered "injustice of things" has been clarified by thinking the essence of what lingers awhile in presence as the disjunction in lingering. The disjunction consists in the fact that whatever lingers awhile seeks to win for itself a while based solely on the model of continuance. Lingering as persisting, considered with respect to the jointure of the while, is an insurrection on behalf of sheer endurance. Continuance asserts itself in presencing as such, which lets each present being linger awhile in the expanse of unconcealment. In this rebellious whiling whatever lingers awhile insists upon sheer continuance. What is present then comes to presence without, and in opposition to, the jointure of the while. The fragment does not say that whatever is present for the time being loses itself in disjunction; it says that whatever lingers awhile with a view to disjunction διδόναι δίκην, gives jointure.

What does "give" mean here? How should whatever lingers awhile, whatever comes to presence in disjunction, be able to give jointure? Can it give what it doesn't have? If it gives anything at all, doesn't it give jointure away? Where and how does that which is present for the time being give jointure? We must ask our question more clearly, by questioning from within the matter.

How should what is present as such give the jointure of its presencing? The giving designated here can only consist in its manner of presencing. Giving is not only giving-away; originally, giving has the sense of acceding or giving-to. Such giving lets something belong to another which properly belongs to him. What belongs to that which is present is the jointure of its while, which it articulates in its approach and withdrawal. In the jointure whatever lingers awhile keeps to its while. It does not incline toward the disjunction of sheer persistence. The jointure belongs to whatever lingers awhile, which in turn belongs in the jointure. The jointure is order.

Δίκη, thought on the basis of Being as presencing, is the ordering and enjoining Order. Ἀδικία, disjunction, is Disorder. Now it is only necessary that we think this capitalized word capitally—in its full linguistic power.

Whatever lingers awhile in presence comes to presence insofar as it lingers; all the while, emerging and passing away, and the jointure of the transition from approach to withdrawal, continue. This lingering endurance of the transition is the enjoined continuance of what is present. The enjoined continuance does not at all insist upon sheer persistence. It does not fall into disjunction; it surmounts disorder. Lingering the length of its while, whatever lingers awhile lets its essence as presencing belong to order. The διδόναι designates this "letting belong to."

The presencing of whatever is present for the time being does not consist in ἀδικία by itself, i.e. not in disorder alone; rather, it consists in διδόναι δίκην . . . τῆς ἀδικίας, since whatever is present lets order belong in each case. Whatever is presently present is not a slice of something shoved in between what is not presently present; it is present insofar as it lets itself belong to the non-present:

$$\text{διδόναι . . . αὐτὰ δίκην . . . τῆς ἀδικίας,}$$

—they, these same beings, let order belong (by the surmounting) of disorder.

The experience of beings in their Being which here comes to language is neither pessimistic nor nihilistic; nor is it optimistic. It is tragic. That is a presumptuous thing to say. However, we discover a trace of the essence of tragedy, not when we explain it psychologically or aesthetically, but rather only when we consider its essential form, the Being of beings, by thinking the διδόναι δίκην . . . τῆς ἀδικίας.

Whatever lingers awhile in presence, τὰ ἐόντα, becomes present when it lets enjoining order belong. To what does the order of jointure belong, and where does it belong? When and in what way does that which lingers awhile in presence give order? The fragment does not directly say anything about this, at least to the extent we have so far considered it. If we turn our attention to the still untranslated portion, however, it seems to say clearly to whom or what the διδόναι is directed:

$$\text{διδόναι γὰρ αὐτὰ δίκην καὶ τίσιν ἀλλήλοις}$$

—present beings which linger awhile let order belong ἀλλήλοις, to one

44

another. Thus we are generally accustomed to read the text; we relate
the ἀλλήλοις to δίκην and τίσιν, if we represent it clearly and expressly name it, as does Diels—though Nietzsche passes over it entirely in his translation. However, it seems to me that the immediate
relation of ἀλλήλοις to διδόναι δίκην is neither linguistically necessary nor, more important, justified by the matter itself. Therefore it
remains for us to ask, from within the matter itself, whether ἀλλήλοις
should be directly related also to δίκην, or whether it should not
indeed rather be related only to the τίσιν which immediately precedes
it. The decision in this case depends in part on how we translate the
καί that stands between δίκην and τίσιν. But this is determined by
what τίσις here says.

We usually translate τίσις by "penalty." This leads us to translate
διδόναι as "to pay." Whatever lingers awhile in presence pays penalty;
it expends this as its punishment (δίκη). The court of justice is com-
plete. It lacks nothing, not even injustice—though of course no one
rightly knows what might constitute injustice.

Surely, τίσις can mean penalty, but it must not, because the
original and essential significance of the word is not thereby named.
For τίσις is "esteem" [*Schätzen*]. To esteem something means to heed
it, and so to take satisfactory care of what is estimable in it. The essential process of esteem, which is to satisfy, can, in what is good, be a
magnamimous action; but with respect to wickedness giving satisfac-
tion may mean paying a penalty. Yet a mere commentary on the word
does not bring us to the matter in the fragment's use of the word if we
have not already, as with ἀδικία and δίκη, thought from within the
matter which comes to language in the fragment.

According to the fragment the αὐτά (τὰ ἐόντα), those beings that
linger awhile in presence, stand in disorder. As they linger awhile,
they tarry. They hang on. For they advance hesitantly through their
while, in transition from arrival to departure. They hang on; they cling
to themselves. When what lingers awhile delays, it stubbornly follows
the inclination to persist in hanging on, and indeed to insist on persisting; it aims at everlasting continuance and no longer bothers about
δίκη, the order of the while.

But in this way everything that lingers awhile strikes a haughty pose toward every other of its kind. None heeds the lingering presence of the others. Whatever lingers awhile is inconsiderate toward others, each dominated by what is implied in its lingering presence, namely, the craving to persist. Beings which linger awhile do not in this respect simply drift into inconsiderateness. Inconsiderateness impels them toward persistence, so that they may still present themselves as what is present. Nevertheless, what is present in totality does not simply disintegrate into inconsiderate individualities; it does not dissipate itself in discontinuity. Rather, the saying now says:

$$\delta\iota\delta\acute{o}\nu\alpha\iota \ldots \tau\acute{\iota}\sigma\iota\nu \ \acute{\alpha}\lambda\lambda\acute{\eta}\lambda o\iota\varsigma$$

—beings which linger awhile let belong, one to the other: consideration with regard to one another. The translation of τίσις as consideration coincides better with the essential meaning of "heeding" and "esteeming." It is thought from within the matter, on the basis of the presencing of what lingers awhile. But the word "consideration" means for us too directly that human trait, while τίσις is applied neutrally, because more essentially, to everything present, αὐτά (τὰ ἐόντα). Our word "consideration" lacks not only the necessary breadth, but above all the gravity to speak as the translating word for τίσις in the fragment, and as the word corresponding to δίκη, order.

Now our language possesses an old word which, interestingly enough, we moderns know only in its negative form, indeed only as a form of disparagement, as with the word *Unfug* [disorder]. This usually suggests to us something like an improper or vulgar sort of behavior, something perpetrated in a crude manner. In the same fashion, we still use the word *ruchlos* [reckless] to mean something pejorative and shameful: something without *Ruch* [reck]. We no longer really know what *Ruch* means. The Middle High German word *ruoche* means solicitude or care. Care tends to something so that it may remain in its essence. This turning-itself-toward, when thought of what lingers awhile in relation to presencing, is τίσις, reck. Our word *geruhen* [to deign or respect] is related to reck and has nothing to do with *Ruhe* [rest]: to deign means to esteem something, to let or allow something to be itself. What we observed concerning the word "consideration," that it has to do with human relations, is also true of *ruoche*. But we shall take advantage of the obsolescence of the word by adopting it anew in its essential breadth; we will speak of τίσις as the reck corresponding to δίκη, order.

Insofar as beings which linger awhile do not entirely dissipate themselves in the boundless conceit of aiming for a baldly insistent subsistence, insofar as they no longer share the compulsion to expel one another from what is presently present, they let order belong, διδόναι δίκην. Insofar as beings which linger awhile give order, each being thereby lets reck belong to the other, lets reck pervade its relations with the others, διδόναι . . . καὶ τίσιν ἀλλήλοις. Only when we have already thought τὰ ἐόντα as what is present, and this as the totality of what lingers awhile, does ἀλλήλοις receive the significance thought for it in the fragment: within the open expanse of unconcealment each lingering being becomes present to every other being. So long as we do not think of the τὰ ἐόντα, the ἀλλήλοις remains a name for an indeterminate reciprocity in a chaotic manifold. The more strictly we think in ἀλλήλοις the manifold of beings lingering awhile, the clearer becomes the necessary relation of ἀλλήλοις to τίσις. The more unequivocally this relation emerges, the more clearly we recognize that the διδόναι . . . τίσιν ἀλλήλοις, each one giving reck to the other, is the sole manner in which what lingers awhile in presence lingers at all, i.e. διδόναι δίκην, granting order. The καί between δίκην and τίσιν is not simply the vacuous conjunction "and." It signifies the essential process. If what is present grants order, it happens in this manner: as beings linger awhile, they give reck to one another. The surmounting of disorder properly occurs through the letting-belong of reck. This means that the essential process of the disorder of non-reck, of the reckless, occurs in ἀδικία:

δίδόναι . . . αὐτὰ δίκην καὶ τίσιν ἀλλήλοις τῆς ἀδικίας

—they let order belong, and thereby also reck, to one another (in the surmounting) of disorder.

To let belong is, as the καί suggests, something twofold, since the essence of ἐόντα is dually determined. Whatever lingers awhile comes to presence from the jointure between approach and withdrawal. It comes to presence in the "between" of a twofold absence. Whatever lingers awhile comes to presence in each case in accordance with its while. It comes to presence as what is present at the present time. With a view to its while it gives reck, and even a while, to the others. But to whom does whatever is present let the order of jointure belong?

The second clause of the fragment, which we have been interpreting, does not answer this question. But it provides a clue. For we have passed over a word: διδόναι γὰρ αὐτά . . . they (namely) let belong. . . . The γάρ, "for" or "namely," introduces a grounding. In any case, the second clause delineates the extent to which the matter of the previous clause behaves in the prescribed manner.

What does the translation of the fragment's second clause say? It says that the ἐόντα, whatever is present, as that which lingers awhile, is released into reckless disorder; and it tells how present beings surmount disorder by letting order and reck belong to one another. This letting-belong is the manner in which what lingers awhile lingers and so comes to presence as what is present. The fragment's second clause designates what is present in the manner of its presencing. The saying speaks of what is present and tells about its presencing. This it places in the brilliance of what is thought. The second clause offers a commentary on the presencing of what is present.

For this reason the first clause must designate presencing itself, and even the extent to which presencing determines what is present as such; only so can the second clause in turn, referring back to the first by means of the γάρ, comment on the presencing of what is present. Presencing, in relation to what is present, is always that in accordance with which what is present comes to presence. The first clause names that presencing "in accordance with which . . ." Only the last three words of the first clause are preserved:

$$\text{. . . κατὰ τὸ χρεών·}$$

This is translated: ". . . according to necessity;". We will leave τὸ χρεών untranslated at first. But we can still reflect on two matters concerning τὸ χρεών which arose in our commentary on the second clause and its reference back to the first clause. First, that it designates the presencing of what is present; second, that if χρεών thinks the presencing of what is present, then presencing may be thought somehow in terms of what is present; or it may prove to be otherwise, that the relation of Being to beings can only come from Being, can only rest in the essence of Being.

The word κατά precedes τὸ χρεών. It means "down here from above," or "over here." The κατά refers back to something from which something lower comes to presence, as from something higher and as its consequent. That in reference to which the κατά is pronounced retains something that has befallen it [*Gefälle*], in accordance with which such and such is the case, both for it and for others.

But in consequence of what, or by what befalling, can what is present become present as such, if not in consequence of, or by the befalling of, presencing? That which lingers awhile in presence lingers κατὰ τὸ χρεών. No matter how we are to think τὸ χρεών, the word is the earliest name for what we have thought as the ἐόν of ἐόντα; τὸ χρεών is the oldest name in which thinking brings the Being of beings to language.

That which lingers awhile in presence becomes present as it surmounts reckless disorder, ἀδικία, which haunts lingering itself as an essential possibility. The presencing of what is present *is* such a surmounting. It is accomplished when beings which linger awhile let order belong, and thereby reck, among one another. The answer to the question to whom order belongs is now provided: order belongs to that which comes to presence by way of presencing—and that means by way of a surmounting. Order is κατὰ τὸ χρεών. At this point something of the essence of χρεών begins to glimmer, though at first from a great distance. If, as the essence of presencing, χρεών is related essentially to what is present, then τὸ χρεών must enjoin order and thereby also reck in that relation. The χρεών enjoins matters in such a way that whatever is present lets order and reck belong. The χρεών lets such enjoining prevail among present beings and so grants them the manner of their arrival—as the while of whatever lingers awhile.

What is present comes to presence when it surmounts the dis- of disorder, the ἀ– of ἀδικία. This ἀπό in ἀδικία corresponds to the κατά of χρεών. The transitional γάρ in the second clause strings the bow, connecting one end to the other.

So far we have tried to think what τὸ χρεών means only in terms of the reference of the fragment's second clause back to it, without asking about the word itself. What does τὸ χρεών mean? This first word in the fragment's text we are interpreting last because it is first with respect to the matter. What matter? The matter of the presencing of what is present. But to be the Being *of* beings is the matter of Being.

The grammatical form of this enigmatic, ambiguous genitive indicates a genesis, the emergence of what is present from presencing. Yet the essence of this emergence remains concealed along with the essence of these two words. Not only that, but even the very relation between presencing and what is present remains unthought. From early on it seems as though presencing and what is present were each something for itself. Presencing itself unnoticeably becomes something present. Represented in the manner of something present, it is elevated above whatever else is present and so becomes the highest being present. As soon as presencing is named it is represented as some present being. Ultimately, presencing as such is not distinguished from what is present: it is taken merely as the most universal or the highest of present beings, thereby becoming one among such beings. The essence of presencing, and with it the distinction between presencing and what is present, remains forgotten. *The oblivion of Being is oblivion of the distinction between Being and beings.*

However, oblivion of the distinction is by no means the consequence of a forgetfulness of thinking. Oblivion of Being belongs to the self-veiling essence of Being. It belongs so essentially to the destiny of Being that the dawn of this destiny rises as the unveiling of what is present in its presencing. This means that the history of Being begins with the oblivion of Being, since Being—together with its essence, its distinction from beings—keeps to itself. The distinction collapses. It remains forgotten. Although the two parties to the distinction, what is present and presencing, reveal themselves, they do not do so *as* distinguished. Rather, even the early trace of the distinction is obliterated when presencing appears as something present and finds itself in the position of being the highest being present.

The oblivion of the distinction, with which the destiny of Being begins and which it will carry through to completion, is all the same not a lack, but rather the richest and most prodigious event: in it the history of the Western world comes to be borne out. It is the event of metaphysics. What now *is* stands in the shadow of the already foregone destiny of Being's oblivion.

However, the distinction between Being and beings, as something forgotten, can invade our experience only if it has already unveiled itself with the presencing of what is present; only if it has left a trace which remains preserved in the language to which Being comes. Thinking along those lines, we may surmise that the distinction has been illuminated more in that early word about Being than in recent ones; yet at no time has the distinction been designated as such. Illumination of the distinction therefore cannot mean that the distinction appears as a distinction. On the contrary, the relation to what is present in presencing as such may announce itself in such a way that presencing comes to speak *as this relation.*

The early word concerning Being, τὸ χρεών, designates such a relation. However, we would be deceiving ourselves if we thought we could locate the distinction and get behind its essence merely by etymologically dissecting the meaning of the word χρεών with enough persistence. Perhaps only when we experience historically what has not been thought—the oblivion of Being—as what is to be thought, and only when we have for the longest time pondered what we have long experienced in terms of the destiny of Being, may the early word speak in our contemporary recollection.

We are accustomed to translate the word χρεών by "necessity." By that we mean what is compelling—that which inescapably must be. Yet we err if we adhere to this derived meaning exclusively. Χρεών is derived from χράω, χράομαι. It suggests ἡ χείρ, the hand; χράω means: I get involved with something, I reach for it, extend my hand to it. At the same time χράω means to place in someone's hands or hand over, thus to deliver, to let something belong to someone. But such delivery is of a kind which keeps this transfer in hand, and with it what is transferred.

Therefore the participial χρεών originally signifies nothing of constraint and of what "must be." Just as little does the word initially or ever mean to ratify and ordain.

If we firmly keep in mind that we must think the word within the Anaximander fragment, then it can only mean what is essential in the presencing *of* what is present, and hence that relation to which the genitive so mysteriously alludes. Τὸ χρεών is thus the handing over of presence which presencing delivers to what is present, and which thus keeps in hand, i.e. preserves in presencing, what is present as such.

The relation to what is present that rules in the essence of presencing itself is a unique one, altogether incomparable to any other relation. It belongs to the uniqueness of Being itself. Therefore, in order to name the essential nature of Being, language would have to find a single word, the unique word. From this we can gather how daring every thoughtful word addressed to Being is. Nevertheless such daring is not impossible, since Being speaks always and everywhere throughout language. The difficulty lies not so much in finding in thought the word for Being as in retaining purely in genuine thinking the word found.

Anaximander says, τὸ χρεών. We will dare a translation which sounds strange and which can be easily misinterpreted: τὸ χρεών, usage [*der Brauch*].

With this translation we ascribe to the Greek word a sense that is foreign neither to the word itself nor to the matter designated by the word in the saying. Nonetheless the translation makes excessive demands. It loses none of this character even when we consider that all translation in the field of thinking inevitably makes such demands.

To what extent is τὸ χρεών "usage"? The strangeness of the translation is reduced when we think more clearly about the word in our language. Usually we understand "to use" to mean utilizing and benefiting from what we have a right to use. What our utilizing benefits from becomes the usual. Whatever is used is in usage. "Usage," as the word that translates τὸ χρεών, should not be understood in these current, derived senses. We should rather keep to the root-meaning: to use is to brook [*bruchen*], in Latin *frui,* in German *fruchten, Frucht.* * We translate this freely as "to enjoy," which originally means to be pleased with something and so to have it in use. Only in its derived senses does "enjoy" mean simply to consume or gobble up. We encounter what we have called the basic meaning of "use," in the sense of *frui,* in Augustine's words, *Quid enim est aliud quod dicimus frui, nisi praesto habēre, quod diligis?* ** *Frui* involves *praesto habēre. Praesto, praesitum* is in Greek ὑποκείμενον, that which already lies before us in unconcealment, οὐσία, that which lingers awhile in presence. "To use" accordingly suggests: to let something present come to presence as such; *frui,* to brook, to use, usage, means: to hand something over to its own essence and to keep it in hand, preserving it as something present.

In the translation of τὸ χρεών usage is thought as essential presencing in Being itself. "To brook," *frui,* is no longer merely predicated of enjoyment as a form of human behavior; nor is it said in relation to any being whatsoever, even the highest *(fruitio Dei* as the *beatitudo hominis);* rather, usage now designates the manner in which Being itself presences as the relation to what is present, approaching and becoming involved with what is present as present: τὸ χρεών.

Usage delivers what is present to its presencing, i.e. to its lingering. Usage dispenses to what is present the portion of its while. The while apportioned in each case to what lingers rests in the jointure which joins what is present in the transition between twofold absence (arrival and departure). The jointure of the while bounds and confines what is present as such. That which lingers awhile in presence, τὰ ἐόντα, comes to presence within bounds (πέρας).

*"To brook" is today used only in negative constructions—"I'll brook no rival!"—which suggest unwillingness to put up with a state of affairs. It shares its original Teutonic stem with the modern German *brauchen* and the Middle High German *brûchen: bruk-,* from the Indo-European *bhrug-.* Its archaic senses include: to make use of, to have the enjoyment of, to bear or hold, to possess the right of usufruct—i.e. the right to cultivate and use land one does not own, and to enjoy its fruits.—Tr.

**"For what else do we mean when we say *frui* if not to have at hand something that is especially prized?" *De moribus ecclesiae,* lib. I, c. 3; cf. *De doctrina christiana,* lib. I, c. 2-4. For the first see *Basic Writings of Saint Augustine,* 2 vols., ed. Whitney J. Oates (New York: Random House, 1948) I, 321; for the second see *On Christian Doctrine,* trans. D. W. Robertson, Jr. (New York: Liberal Arts Press, 1958), pp. 9-10.—Tr.

As dispenser of portions of the jointure, usage is the fateful join-ing: the enjoining of order and thereby of reck. Usage distributes order and reck in such manner that it reserves for itself what is meted out, gathers it to itself, and secures it as what is present in presencing.

But usage, enjoining order and so limiting what is present, distributes boundaries. As τὸ χρεών it is therefore at the same time ἄπειρον, that which is without boundary, since its essence consists in sending boundaries of the while to whatever lingers awhile in pres-ence.

According to the tradition recounted in Simplicius' commentary on Aristotle's *Physics*, Anaximander is supposed to have said that what-ever is present has its essential origin in what presences without bounds: ἀρχὴ τῶν ὄντων τὸ ἄπειρον. What presences without bounds, not joined by order and reck, is not some present being but rather τὸ χρεών.

Enjoining order and reck, usage delivers to each present being the while into which it is released. But accompanying this process is the constant danger that lingering will petrify into mere persistence. Thus usage essentially remains at the same time the distribution of presenc-ing into disorder. Usage conjoins the dis-.

Therefore, whatever lingers awhile in presence can only come to presence when it lets order and thereby also reck belong: with respect to usage. What is present comes to presence κατὰ τὸ χρεών, along the lines of usage. Usage is the enjoining and preserving gathering of what is present in its presencing, a presencing which lingers awhile accord-ing to each particular case.

The translation of τὸ χρεών as "usage" has not resulted from a preoccupation with etymologies and dictionary meanings. The choice of the word stems from a prior crossing *over* of a thinking which tries to think the distinction in the essence of Being in the fateful beginning of Being's oblivion. The word "usage" is dictated to thinking in the ex-perience of Being's oblivion. What properly remains to be thought in the word "usage" has presumably left a trace in τὸ χρεών. This trace quickly vanishes in the destiny of Being which unfolds in world history as Western metaphysics.

The Anaximander fragment, thinking of what is present in its presencing, elucidates what τὸ χρεών means. What is thought as χρεών in the fragment is the first and most thoughtful interpretation of what the Greeks experienced in the name Μοῖρα as the dispensing of portions. Gods and men are subordinated to Μοῖρα. Τὸ Χρεών, usage, is the handing over of what is in each case present into its while in unconcealment.

Τὸ Χρεών harbors the still hidden essence of the gathering which clears and shelters. Usage is the gathering: ὁ Λόγος. From the essence of Λόγος, thought in this way, the essence of Being is determined as the unifying One, Ἕν. Parmenides thinks this same Ἕν. He thinks the unity of this unifying One expressly as the Μοῖρα (fr. VIII, 37). Thought from within the essential experience of Being, Μοῖρα corresponds to the Λόγος of Heraclitus. The essence of Μοῖρα and Λόγος is thoughtfully intimated in the Χρεών of Anaximander.

To search for influences and dependencies among thinkers is to misunderstand thinking. Every thinker is dependent—upon the address of Being. The extent of this dependence determines the freedom from irrelevant influences. The broader the dependence the more puissant the freedom of thought, and therefore the more foreboding the danger that it may wander past what was once thought, and yet —perhaps only thus—think the Same.

Of course, in our recollecting we latecomers must first have thought about the Anaximander fragment in order to proceed to the thought of Parmenides and Heraclitus. If we have done so, then the misinterpretation that the philosophy of the former must have been a doctrine of Being while that of the latter was a doctrine of Becoming is exposed as superficial.

However, in order to think the Anaximander fragment we must first of all, but then continually, take a simple step: we must cross over to what that always unspoken word, ἐόν, ἐόντα, εἶναι says. It says: presencing into unconcealment. Concealed in that word is this: *presencing brings unconcealment along with itself.* Unconcealment itself is presencing. Both are the Same, though they are not identical.

What is present is that which, whether presently or not, presences in unconcealment. Along with the Ἀλήθεια which belongs to the essence of Being, the Λήθη remains entirely unthought, as in consequence do "presently" and "non-presently," i.e. the region of the open expanse in which everything present arrives and in which the presencing to one another of beings which linger awhile is unfolded and delimited.

Because beings are what is present in the manner of that which lingers awhile, once they have arrived in unconcealment they can linger there, they can appear. Appearance is an essential consequence of presencing and of the kind of presencing involved. Only what appears can in the first place show an aspect and form, thinking these matters always from within presencing. Only a thinking which has beforehand thought Being in the sense of presencing into unconcealment can think the presencing of what is present as ἰδέα. But whatever lingers awhile in presence at the same time lingers as something brought forward into unconcealment. It is so brought when, arising by itself, it produces itself; or it is so brought when it is produced by man. In both cases what has arrived in the foreground of unconcealment is in a certain sense an ἔργον, which in Greek is thought as something brought forward. The presencing of what is present, with respect to its ἔργον character, thought in the light of presence, can be experienced as that which occurs essentially in production. This is the presencing of what is present: the Being of beings is ἐνέργεια.

The ἐνέργεια which Aristotle thinks as the fundamental character of presencing, of ἐόν, the ἰδέα which Plato thinks as the fundamental character of presencing, the Λόγος which Heraclitus thinks as the fundamental character of presencing, the Μοῖρα which Parmenides thinks as the fundamental character of presencing, the Χρεών which Anaximander thinks is essential in presencing—all these name the Same. In the concealed richness of the Same the unity of the unifying One, the Ἕν, is thought by each thinker in his own way.

Meanwhile an epoch of Being soon comes in which ἐνέργεια is translated as *actualitas*. The Greek is shut away, and to the present day the word appears only in Roman type. *Actualitas* becomes *Wirklichkeit* [reality]. Reality becomes objectivity [*Objektivität*]. But objectivity must still preserve the character of presencing if it is to remain in its essence, its objectivity [*Gegenständlichkeit*]. It is the "presence"

[*Präsenz*] of representational thinking. The decisive turn in the destiny of Being as ἐνέργεια lies in the transition to *actualitas*.

Could a mere translation have precipitated all this? We may yet learn what can come to pass in translation. The truly fateful encounter with historic language is a silent event. But in it the destiny of Being speaks. Into what language is the land of evening translated?

We shall now try to translate the Anaximander fragment:

. . . κατὰ τὸ χρεών· διδόναι γὰρ αὐτὰ δίκην καὶ τίσιν ἀλλήλοις τῆς ἀδικίας.

. . . along the lines of usage; for they let order and thereby also reck belong to one another (in the surmounting) of disorder.

We cannot demonstrate the adequacy of the translation by scholarly means; nor should we simply accept it through faith in some authority or other. Scholarly proof will not carry us far enough, and faith has no place in thinking. We can only reflect on the translation by thinking through the saying. But thinking is the poetizing of the truth of Being in the historic dialogue between thinkers.

For this reason the fragment will never engage us so long as we only explain it historiologically and philologically. Curiously enough, the saying first resonates when we set aside the claims of our own familiar ways of representing things, as we ask ourselves in what the confusion of the contemporary world's fate consists.

Man has already begun to overwhelm the entire earth and its atmosphere, to arrogate to himself in forms of energy the concealed powers of nature, and to submit future history to the planning and ordering of a world government. This same defiant man is utterly at a loss simply to say what *is;* to say *what* this *is*—that a thing *is*.

The totality of beings is the single object of a singular will to conquer. The simplicity of Being is confounded in a singular oblivion.

What mortal can fathom the abyss of this confusion? He may try to shut his eyes before this abyss. He may entertain one delusion after another. The abyss does not vanish.

Theories of nature and doctrines of history do not dissolve the confusion. They further confuse everything until it is unrecognizable, since they themselves feed on the confusion prevailing over the distinction between beings and Being.

Is there any rescue? Rescue comes when and only when danger *is*. Danger *is* when Being itself advances to its farthest extreme, and when the oblivion that issues from Being itself undergoes reversal.

But what if Being in its essence *needs to use* [*braucht*] the essence of man? If the essence of man consists in thinking the truth of Being?

Then thinking must poetize on the riddle of Being. It brings the dawn of thought into the neighborhood of what is for thinking.

TWO

Logos
(Heraclitus, Fragment B 50)

The path most needed for our thinking stretches far ahead. It leads to that simple matter which, under the name λόγος, remains for thinking. Yet there are only a few signs to point out the way.

By means of free reflection along the guidelines of a saying of Heraclitus (B 50), the following essay attempts to take a few steps along that path. Perhaps they can carry us to the point where at least this one saying will speak to us in a more question-worthy way:

> οὐκ ἐμοῦ ἀλλὰ τοῦ Λόγου ἀκούσαντας
> ὁμολογεῖν σοφόν ἐστιν῾Εν Πάντα.

One among the virtually identical translations reads:

> When you have listened not to me but to the Meaning,
> it is wise within the same Meaning to say: *One* is All.
> (Snell)

The saying speaks of ἀκούειν, hearing and having heard, of ὁμολογεῖν, to say the same, of Λόγος, what is said and the saying, of ἐγώ, the thinker himself as λέγων, the one who is talking. Heraclitus here considers a hearing and a saying. He expresses what the Λόγος says: ῾Εν Πάντα, all is One. The saying of Heraclitus seems comprehensible in every respect. Nevertheless, everything about it is worthy of question. Most question-worthy is what is most self-evident, namely, our presupposition that whatever Heraclitus says ought to

become immediately obvious to our contemporary everyday understanding. This demand was probably never met even for Heraclitus'
contemporaries.

In the meantime, we would correspond sooner to his thinking if
we conceded that several riddles remain, neither for the first time with
us, nor only for the ancients, but rather in the very matter thought. We
will get closer to these riddles if we step back before them. That done,
it becomes clear that in order to observe the riddle as a riddle we must
clarify before all else what λόγος and λέγειν mean.

Since antiquity the Λόγος of Heraclitus has been interpreted in
various ways: as *Ratio,* as *Verbum,* as cosmic law, as the logical, as
necessity in thought, as meaning and as reason. Again and again a call
rings out for reason to be the standard for deeds and omissions. Yet
what can reason do when, along with the irrational and the antirational
all on the same level, it perseveres in the same neglect, forgetting to
meditate on the essential origin of reason and to let itself into its
advent? What can logic, λογική (ἐπιστήμη) of any sort, do if we never
begin to pay heed to the Λόγος and follow its primordial essence?

What λόγος is we gather from λέγειν. What does λέγειν mean?
Everyone familiar with the language knows that λέγειν means talking
and saying; λόγος means λέγειν as a saying aloud, and λεγόμενον as
that which is said.

Who would want to deny that in the language of the Greeks from
early on λέγειν means to talk, say, or tell? However, just as early and
even more originally—and therefore already in the previously cited
meaning—it means what our similarly sounding *legen* means: to lay
down and lay before. In *legen* a "bringing together" prevails, the Latin
legere understood as *lesen,* in the sense of collecting and bringing
together. Λέγειν properly means the laying-down and laying-before
which gathers itself and others. The middle voice, λέγεσθαι, means to
lay oneself down in the gathering of rest; λέχος is the resting place;
λόχος is a place of ambush [or a place for lying in wait] where something is laid away and deposited. (The old word ἀλέγω (ἀ
copulativum), archaic after Aeschylus and Pindar, should be recalled
here: something "lies upon me," it oppresses and troubles me.)

All the same it remains incontestable that λέγειν means, predominately if not exclusively, saying and talking. Must we therefore, in deference to this preponderant and customary meaning of λέγειν, which assumes multiple forms, simply toss the genuine meaning of the word, λέγειν as laying, to the winds? Dare we ever do such a thing? Or is it not finally time to engage ourselves with a question which probably decides many things? The question asks: How does the proper sense of λέγειν, to lay, come to mean saying and talking?

In order to find the foothold for an answer, we need to reflect on what actually lies in λέγειν as laying. To lay means to bring to lie. Thus, to lay is at the same time to place one thing beside another, to lay them together. To lay is to gather [*lesen*]. The *lesen* better known to us, namely, the *reading* of something written, remains but one sort of gathering, in the sense of bringing-together-into-lying-before, although it is indeed the predominant sort. The gleaning at harvest time gathers fruit from the soil. The gathering of the vintage involves picking grapes from the vine. Picking and gleaning are followed by the bringing together of the fruit. So long as we persist in the usual appearances we are inclined to take this bringing together as the gathering itself or even its termination. But gathering is more than mere amassing. To gathering belongs a collecting which brings under shelter. Accommodation governs the sheltering; accommodation is in turn governed by safekeeping. That "something extra" which makes gathering more than a jumbling together that snatches things up is not something only added afterward. Even less is it the conclusion of the gathering, coming last. The safekeeping that brings something in has already determined the first steps of the gathering and arranged everything that follows. If we are blind to everything but the sequence of steps, then the collecting follows the picking and gleaning, the bringing under shelter follows the collecting, until finally everything is accommodated in bins and storage rooms. This gives rise to the illusion that preservation and safekeeping have nothing to do with gathering. Yet what would become of a vintage [*eine Lese*] which has not been gathered with an eye to the fundamental matter of its being sheltered? The sheltering [*Bergen*] comes first in the essential formation of the vintage.

However, the sheltering does not secure just any thing that happens along: the gathering which properly begins with the sheltering, i.e. the vintage, is itself from the start a selection [*Auslese*] which requires sheltering. For its part, the selection is determined by whatever within the crop to be sorted shows itself as to-be-selected [*Erlesene*]. The most important aspect of the sheltering in the essential formation of the vintage is the sorting (in Alemanic [the southwestern German dialect]: the fore-gathering [*Vor-lese*]) which determines the selection, arranging everything involved in the bringing together, the bringing under shelter, and the accommodation of the vintage.

The sequence of steps in the gathering act does not coincide with the order of those far-reaching, fundamental traits in which the essence of the vintage [*die Lese*] consists.

It is proper to every gathering that the gatherers assemble to coordinate their work to the sheltering, and—gathered together with that end in view—first begin to gather. The gathering [*die Lese*] requires and demands this assembly. This original coordination governs their collective gathering.

However, *lesen* [to gather] thought in this way does not simply stand near *legen* [to lay]. Nor does the former simply accompany the latter. Rather, gathering is already included in laying. Every gathering is already a laying. Every laying is of itself gathering. Then what does "to lay" mean? Laying brings to lie, in that it lets things lie together before us. All too readily we take this "letting" in the sense of omitting or letting go. To lay, to bring to lie, to let lie, would then mean to concern ourselves no longer with what is laid down and lies before us—to ignore it. However, λέγειν, to lay, by its letting-lie-together-before means just this, that whatever lies before us involves us and therefore concerns us. Laying as letting-lie-together-before [*bei-sammen-vorliegen-Lassen*] is concerned with retaining whatever is laid down as lying before us. (In the Alemanic dialect *legi* means a weir or dam which lies ahead in the river, against the water's current.)

The λέγειν or laying now to be thought has in advance relinquished all claims—claims never even known to it—to be that which for the first time brings whatever lies before us into its position [*Lage*]. Laying, as λέγειν, simply tries to let what of itself lies together here before us, *as* what lies before, into its protection, a protection in which it remains laid down. What sort of protection is this? What lies together before us is stored, laid away, secured and deposited in unconcealment, and that means sheltered in unconcealment. By letting things lie together before us, λέγειν undertakes to secure what lies before us in unconcealment. The κεῖσθαι, the lying before for-itself of what is in this fashion deposited, i.e. the κεῖσθαι of ὑποκείμενον, is nothing more and nothing less than the *presencing* of that which lies before us into unconcealment. In this λέγειν of ὑποκείμενον, λέγειν as gathering and assembling remains implied. Because λέγειν, which lets things lie together before us, concerns itself solely with the safety of that which lies before us in unconcealment, the gathering appropriate to such a laying is determined in advance by safekeeping.

Λέγειν is to lay. Laying is the letting-lie-before—which is gathered into itself—of that which comes together into presence.

The question arises: How does the proper meaning of λέγειν, to lay, attain the signification of saying and talking? The foregoing reflection already contains the answer, for it makes us realize that we can no longer raise the question in such a manner. Why not? Because what we have been thinking about in no way tells us that this word λέγειν advanced from the one meaning, "to lay," to the other, "to say."

We have not busied ourselves in the foregoing with the transformation of word meanings. Rather, we have stumbled upon an event whose immensity still lies concealed in its long unnoticed simplicity.

The saying and talking of mortals comes to pass from early on as λέγειν, laying. Saying and talking occur essentially as the letting-lie-together-before of everything which, laid in unconcealment, comes to presence. The original λέγειν, laying, unfolds itself early and in a manner ruling everything unconcealed as saying and talking. Λέγειν as laying lets itself be overpowered by the predominant sense, but only in order to deposit the essence of saying and talking at the outset under the governance of laying proper.

That λέγειν is a laying wherein saying and talking articulate their essence, refers to the earliest and most consequential decision concerning the essence of language. Where did it come from? This question is as weighty, and supposedly the same, as the other question: How far does this characterization of the essence of language from laying extend? The question reaches into the uttermost of the possible essential origins of language. For, like the letting-lie-before that gathers, saying receives its essential form from the unconcealment of that which lies together before us. But the unconcealing of the concealed into unconcealment is the very presencing of what is present. We call this the Being of beings. Thus, the essential speaking of language, λέγειν as laying, is determined neither by vocalization (φωνή) nor by signifying (σημαίνειν). Expression and signification have long been accepted as manifestations which indubitably betray some characteristics of language. But they do not genuinely reach into the realm of the primordial, essential determination of language, nor are they at all capable of determining this realm in its primary characteristics. That saying as laying ruled unnoticed and from early on, and—as if nothing at all had occurred there—that speaking accordingly appeared as λέγειν, produced a curious state of affairs. Human thought was never astonished by this event, nor did it discern in it a mystery which concealed an essential dispensation of Being to men, a dispensation perhaps reserved for that historical moment which would not only devastate man from top to bottom but send his very essence reeling.

To say is λέγειν. This sentence, if well thought, now sloughs off everything facile, trite, and vacuous. It names the inexhaustible mystery that the speaking of language comes to pass from the unconcealment of what is present, and is determined according to the lying-before of what is present as the letting-lie-together-before. Will thinking finally learn to catch a glimpse of what it means that Aristotle could characterize λέγειν as ἀποφαίνεσθαι? The λόγος by itself brings that which appears and comes forward in its lying before us to appearance—to its luminous self-showing (cf. *Being and Time,* § 7b).

Saying is a letting-lie-together-before which gathers and is gathered. If such is the essence of speaking, then what is hearing? As λέγειν, speaking is not characterized as a reverberation which expresses meaning. If saying is not characterized by vocalization, then neither can the hearing which corresponds to it occur as a reverberation meeting the ear and getting picked up, as sounds troubling the auditory sense and being transmitted. Were our hearing primarily and always only this picking up and transmitting of sounds, conjoined by several other processes, the result would be that the reverberation would go in one ear and out the other. That happens in fact when we are not gathered to what is addressed. But the addressed is itself that which lies before us, as gathered and laid before us. Hearing is actually this gathering of oneself which composes itself on hearing the pronouncement and its claim. Hearing is primarily gathered hearkening. What is heard comes to presence in hearkening. We hear when we are "all ears." But "ear" does not here mean the acoustical sense apparatus. The anatomically and physiologically identifiable ears, as the tools of sensation, never bring about a hearing, not even if we take this solely as an apprehending of noises, sounds, and tones. Such apprehending can neither be anatomically established nor physiologically demonstrated, nor in any way grasped as a biological process at work within the organism—although apprehension lives only so long as it is embodied. So long as we think of hearing along the lines of acoustical science, everything is made to stand on its head. We wrongly think that the activation of the body's audio equipment is hearing proper. But then hearing in the sense of hearkening and heeding is supposed to be a transposition of hearing proper into the realm of the spiritual [*das Geistige*]. In the domain of scientific research one can establish many useful findings. One can demonstrate that periodic oscillations in air pressure of a certain frequency are experienced as tones. From such kinds of determinations concerning what is heard, an investigation can be launched which eventually only specialists in the physiology of the senses can conduct.

In contrast to this, perhaps only a little can be said concerning proper hearing, which nevertheless concerns everyone directly. Here it is not so much a matter for research, but rather of paying thoughtful attention to simple things. Thus, precisely this belongs to proper hearing: that man can hear wrongly insofar as he does not catch what is essential. If the ears do not belong directly to proper hearing, in the sense of hearkening, then hearing and the ears are in a special situation. We do not hear because we have ears. We have ears, i.e. our bodies are equipped with ears, because we hear. Mortals hear the thunder of the heavens, the rustling of woods, the gurgling of fountains, the ringing of plucked strings, the rumbling of motors, the noises of the city—only and only so far as they always already in some way belong to them and yet do not belong to them.

We are all ears when our gathering devotes itself entirely to hearkening, the ears and the mere invasion of sounds being completely forgotten. So long as we only listen to the sound of a word, as the expression of a speaker, we are not yet even listening at all. Thus, in this way we never succeed in having genuinely heard anything at all. But when does hearing succeed? We have heard [*gehört*] when we *belong to* [*gehören*] the matter addressed. The speaking of that which is spoken to is λέγειν, letting-lie-together-before. To belong to speech—this is nothing else than in each case letting whatever a letting-lie-before lays down before us lie gathered in its entirety. Such a letting-lie establishes whatever lies before us as lying-before. It establishes this as itself. It lays one and the Same in one. It lays one as the Same. Such λέγειν lays one and the same, the ὁμόν. Such λέγειν is ὁμολογεῖν: One as the Same, i.e. a letting-lie-before of what does lie before us, gathered in the selfsameness of its lying-before.

Proper hearing occurs essentially in λέγειν as ὁμολογεῖν. This is consequently a λέγειν which lets lie before us whatever already lies together before us; which indeed lies there by virtue of a laying which concerns everything that lies together before us of itself. This exceptional laying is the λέγειν which comes to pass as the Λόγος.

Thus is Λόγος named without qualification: ὁ Λόγος, the Laying: the pure letting-lie-together-before of that which of itself comes to lie before us, in its lying there. In this fashion Λόγος occurs essentially as the pure laying which gathers and assembles. Λόγος is the original assemblage of the primordial gathering from the primordial Laying. Ὁ Λόγος is the Laying that gathers [*die lesende Lege*], and only this.

However, is all this no more than an arbitrary interpretation and an all-too-alien translation with respect to the usual understanding which takes Λόγος as meaning and reason? At first it does sound strange, and it may remain so for a long time—calling Λόγος "the Laying that gathers." But how can anyone decide whether what this translation implies concerning the essence of Λόγος remains appropriate, if only in the most remote way, to what Heraclitus named and thought in the name ὁ Λόγος?

The only way to decide is to consider what Heraclitus himself says in the fragment cited. The saying begins: οὐκ ἐμοῦ . . . It begins with a strict, prohibiting "Not . . ." It refers to the saying and talking of Heraclitus himself. It concerns the hearing of mortals. "Not to me," i.e. not to this one who is talking; you are not to heed the vocalization of his talk. You never hear properly so long as your ears hang upon the sound and flow of a human voice in order to snatch up for yourselves a manner of speaking. Heraclitus begins the saying with a rejection of hearing as nothing but the passion of the ears. But this rejection is founded on a reference to proper hearing.

Οὐκ ἐμοῦ ἀλλὰ . . . Not to me should you listen (as though gaping), but rather . . . mortal hearing must attend to something else. To what? Ἀλλὰ τοῦ Λόγου. The way of proper hearing is determined by the Λόγος. But inasmuch as the Λόγος is named without qualification it cannot be just any customary thing. Therefore, the hearing appropriate to *it* cannot proceed casually toward it, only to pass it by once again. If there is to be proper hearing, mortals must have already heard the Λόγος with an attention [*Gehör*] which implies nothing less than their belonging to the Λόγος.

Οὐκ ἐμοῦ ἀλλὰ τοῦ Λόγου ἀκούσαντας. "When you have listened, not merely to me (the speaker), but rather when you maintain yourselves in hearkening attunement [*Gehören*], then there is proper hearing."

What happens, then, when such hearing occurs? When there is such proper hearing there is ὁμολογεῖν, which can only be what it is as a λέγειν. Proper hearing belongs to the Λόγος. Therefore this hearing is itself a λέγειν. As such, the proper hearing of mortals is in a certain way the Same as the Λόγος. At the same time, however, precisely as ὁμολογεῖν, it is not the Same at all. It is not the same as the Λόγος itself. Rather, ὁμολογεῖν remains a λέγειν which always and only lays or lets lie whatever is already, as ὁμόν, gathered together and lying before us; this lying never springs from the ὁμολογεῖν but rather rests in the Laying that gathers, i.e. in the Λόγος.

But what occurs when there is proper hearing, as ὁμολογεῖν? Heraclitus says: σοφόν ἐστιν. When ὁμολογεῖν occurs, then σοφόν comes to pass. We read: σοφόν ἐστιν. One translates σοφόν correctly as "wise." But what does "wise" mean? Does it mean simply to know in the way old "wise men" know things? What do we know of such knowing? If it remains a having-seen whose seeing is not of the eyes of the senses, just as the having-heard is not hearing with the auditory equipment, then having-seen and having-heard presumably coincide. They do not refer to a mere grasping, but to a certain kind of behavior. Of what sort? Of the sort that maintains itself in the abode of mortals. This abiding holds to what the Laying that gathers lets lie before us, which in each case already lies before us. Thus σοφόν signifies that which can adhere to whatever has been indicated, can devote itself to it, and can dispatch itself toward it (get under way toward it). Because it is appropriate [schickliches] such behavior becomes skillful [geschickt]. When we want to say that someone is particularly skilled at something we still employ such turns of speech as "he has a gift for that and is destined for it." In this fashion we hit upon the genuine meaning of σοφόν, which we translate as "fateful" ["geschicklich"]. But "fateful" from the start says something more than "skillful." When proper hearing, as ὁμολογεῖν, is, then the fateful comes to pass, and mortal λέγειν is dispatched to the Λόγος. It becomes concerned with the Laying that gathers. Λέγειν is dispatched to what is appropriate, to whatever rests in the assemblage of the primordially gathering laying-before, i.e. in that which the Laying that gathers has sent. Thus it is indeed fateful when mortals accomplish proper hearing. But σοφόν is not τὸ Σοφόν, the "fateful" is not "Fate," so called because it gathers to itself all dispensation, and precisely that which is appropriate to the behavior of mortals. We have not yet made out what, according to the thinking of Heraclitus, ὁ Λόγος is; it remains still undecided whether the translation of ὁ Λόγος as "the Laying that gathers" captures even a small part of what the Λόγος is.

And already we face a new riddle: the word τὸ Σοφόν. If we are to think it in Heraclitus' way, we toil in vain so long as we do not pursue it in the saying in which it speaks, up to the very words that conclude it.

Ὁμολογεῖν occurs when the hearing of mortals has become proper hearing. When such a thing happens something fateful comes to pass. Where, and as what, does the fateful presence? Heraclitus says: ὁμολογεῖν σοφόν ἐστιν Ἕν Πάντα, "the fateful comes to pass insofar as One All."

The text which is now current runs: ἓν πάντα εἶναι.* The εἶναι is
an alteration of the sole traditional reading: ἓν πάντα εἰδέναι,
understood to mean, "It is wise to know that everything is one." The
conjectural εἶναι is more appropriate. Still, we set aside the verb. By
what right? Because theῙν Πάντα suffices. But it not only suffices: it
remains far more proper for the matter thought here, and likewise for
the style of Heraclitean speech. Ἑν Πάντα, One: All, All: One.

How easily one speaks these words. How readily they transform
themselves into a stolid maxim. A swarming multiplicity of meanings
nestles in both these dangerously harmless words, ἓν and πάντα. Their
indeterminate juxtaposition permits various assertions. In the words ἓν
πάντα the hasty superficiality of usual representations collides with the
hesitant caution of the thinking that questions. The statement "One is
all" can lend itself to an overhasty account of the world which hopes to
buttress itself with a formula that is in some way correct everywhere,
for all times. But theῙν Πάντα can also conceal a thinker's first steps
which initiate all the following steps in the fateful course of thinking.
The second case applies with Heraclitus' words. We do not know their
content, in the sense of being able to revive Heraclitus' own way of
representing things. We are also far removed from a thoughtful com-
prehension of these words. But from this "far remove" we may still
succeed in delineating more meaningfully a few characteristics of the
scope of the words ἓν and πάντα, and of the phraseῙν Πάντα. This
delineation should remain a free-flowing preliminary sketch rather
than a more self-assured portrayal. Of course, we should attempt such
a sketch only in reflecting upon what Heraclitus said from within the
unity of his saying. As it tells us what and how the fateful is, the saying
names the Λόγος. The saying closes withῙν Πάντα. Is this conclusion
only a termination, or does it first unlock what is to be said, by way of
response?

The usual interpretation understands Heraclitus' fragment thus: it

*See Diels-Kranz, *Die Fragmente der Vorsokratiker*, 6th ed. (Berlin: Weidmannsche Verlagsbuchhandlung, 1951), I, 161, line 17. Kranz rejects the Miller-
Gomperz paraphrase εἰδέναι and prints εἶναι. Heidegger's citation of B 50 capital-
izesῙν Πάντα and drops εἶναι.—TR.

is wise to listen to the pronouncement of the Λόγος and to heed the meaning of what is pronounced, while repeating what one has heard in the statement: One is All. There is the Λόγος. It has something to relate. Then there is also that which it relates, to wit, that everything is one.

However, theῈν Πάντα is not *what* the Λόγος relates as a maxim or gives as a meaning to be understood. ῝Εν Πάντα is not *what* the Λόγος pronounces; rather,῝Εν Πάντα suggests the way in which Λόγος essentially occurs.

῝Εν is the unique One, as unifying. It unifies by assembling. It assembles in that, in gathering, it lets lie before us what lies before us as such and as a whole. The unique One unifies as the Laying that gathers. This gathering and laying unifying assembles all uniting in itself, so that it *is* this One, and as this One, *is* what is unique. Whatever is named῝Εν Πάντα in Heraclitus' fragment gives us a simple clue concerning what the Λόγος is.

Do we wander off the path if we think Λόγος as Λέγειν *prior to* all profound metaphysical interpretations, thereby thinking to establish seriously that Λέγειν, as gathering letting-lie-together-before, can be nothing other than the essence of unification, which assembles everything in the totality of simple presencing? There is only *one* appropriate answer to the question of what Λόγος is. In our formulation it reads: ὁ Λόγος λέγει. Λόγος lets-lie-together-before. What? Πάντα. What this word means Heraclitus tells us immediately and unequivocally in the beginning of fragment B 7: Εἰ πάντα τά ὄντα . . . "If everything (namely) which is present . . ." The Laying that gathers has, as Λόγος, laid down everything present in unconcealment. To lay is to secure. Laying secures everything present in its presencing, from which whatever lingers awhile in presence can be appropriately collected and brought forward by mortal λέγειν. Λόγος lays that which is present before and down into presencing, that is, it puts those things back. Presencing nevertheless suggests: *having come forward to endure in unconcealment.* Because the Λόγος lets lie before us what lies before us as such, it discloses what is present in its presencing. But disclosure is ᾿Αλήθεια. This and Λόγος are the Same. Λέγειν lets ἀληθέα, unconcealment as such, lie before us (cf. B 112*). All disclosure releases what is present from concealment. Disclosure needs concealment. The Ἀ-Λήθεια rests in Λήθη, drawing from it and laying before us whatever remains deposited in Λήθη. Λόγος is *in itself and at the same time* a revealing and a concealing. It is Ἀλήθεια. Unconcealment needs concealment, Λήθη, as a reservoir upon which disclosure can, as it were, draw. Λόγος, the Laying that gathers, has in itself this revealing-concealing character. When we can see in Λόγος how the Ἕν essentially occurs as unifying, it becomes equally clear that this unifying which occurs in the Λόγος remains infinitely different from what we tend to represent as a connecting or binding together. The unifying that rests in λέγειν is neither a mere comprehensive collecting nor a mere coupling of opposites which equalizes all contraries. The Ἕν Πάντα lets lie together before us in one presencing things which are usually separated from, and opposed to, one another, such as day and night, winter and summer, peace and war, waking and sleeping, Dionysos and Hades. Such opposites, borne along the farthest distance between presence and absence, διαφερόμενον, let the Laying that gathers lie before us in its full bearing. Its laying is itself that which carries things along by bearing them out. The Ἕν is itself a carrying out.

Ἕν Πάντα says what the Λόγος is. Λόγος says how Ἕν Πάντα essentially occurs. Both are the Same.

When mortal λέγειν is dispatched to the Λόγος, ὁμολογεῖν occurs. This is assembled in the Ἕν, with its unifying dominance. When ὁμολογεῖν occurs, the fateful comes to pass. However, ὁμολογεῖν is never properly Fate itself. Where do we ever find, not merely things that are fated, but *the* fateful itself? What is the fateful

*Fragment B 112, Diels-Kranz I, 176 reads:

σωφρονεῖν ἀρετὴ μεγίστη, καὶ σοφίη ἀληθέα λέγειν καὶ ποιεῖν κατὰ φύσιν ἐπαΐοντας.

Healthful thinking is the greatest perfection; and wisdom consists in saying the truth and acting in accordance with nature, listening to it.

If we may venture another translation: "Thinking is the greatest *areté*, for what is fateful comes to pass when, in dedicated hearkening, we let unconcealment lie before us and bring forth [what is present] along the lines of self-disclosure."—TR.

itself? Heraclitus says what it is unequivocally at the beginning of fragment B 32: Ἕν τὸ σοφὸν μοῦνον, "the unique One unifying all is alone the fateful." But if the Ἕν is the same as the Λόγος, the result is: ὁ Λόγος τὸ σοφὸν μοῦνον. The *only properly* fateful matter is the Λόγος. When mortal λέγειν, as ὁμολογεῖν, is dispatched toward what is fateful, it is sent on its fated way.

But how is Λόγος the fateful, how is it destiny proper, that is, the assembly of that which sends everything into its own? The Laying that gathers assembles in itself all destiny by bringing things and letting them lie before us, keeping each absent and present being in its place and on its way; and by its assembling it secures everything in the totality. Thus each being can be joined and sent into its own. Heraclitus says (B 64): τὰ δὲ Πάντα οἰακίζει Κεραυνός. "But lightning steers (in presencing) the totality (of what is present)."

Lightning abruptly lays before us in an instant everything present in the light of its presencing. The lightning named here steers. It brings all things forward to their designated, essential place. Such instantaneous bringing is the Laying that gathers, the Λόγος. "Lightning" appears here as an epithet of Zeus. As the highest of gods, Zeus is cosmic destiny. The Λόγος, the Ἕν Πάντα, would accordingly be nothing other than the highest god. The essence of Λόγος thus would offer a clue concerning the divinity of the god.

Ought we now to place Λόγος, Ἕν Πάντα, and Ζεύς all together, and even assert that Heraclitus teaches pantheism? Heraclitus does not teach this or any doctrine. As a thinker, he only gives us to think. With regard to our question whether Λόγος (Ἕν Πάντα) and Ζεύς are the Same, he certainly gives us difficult matters to think about. The representational thought of subsequent centuries and millennia has carried this question along without thinking it, ultimately to relieve itself of this unfamiliar burden with the aid of a ready forgetfulness. Heraclitus says (B 32):

Ἕν τὸ Σοφὸν μοῦνον λέγεσθαι οὐκ ἐθέλει
καὶ ἐθέλει Ζηνὸς ὄνομα·

The One, which alone is wise, does not want
and yet does want to be called by the name Zeus.

(Diels-Kranz)

The word that carries the saying, ἐθέλω, does not mean "to want," but rather "to be ready of itself for . . ."; ἐθέλω does not mean merely to demand something, but rather to allow something a reference back to itself. However, if we are to consider carefully the import of what is said in the saying, we must weigh what it says in the first line: Ἐν . . . λέγεσθαι οὐκ ἐθέλει. "The unique-unifying-One, the Laying that gathers, is not ready . . ." Ready for what? For λέγεσθαι, to be assembled under the name "Zeus." For if in such assemblage the Ἐν should be brought to light as Zeus, then perhaps it would always have to remain an apparition. That the saying under consideration concerns λέγεσθαι in immediate relation to ὄνομα (the naming word), indisputably points to the meaning of λέγειν as saying, talking, naming. So precisely this saying of Heraclitus, which seems to contradict directly everything said above concerning λέγειν and λόγος, is designed to allow us renewed thinking on whether and how far λέγειν in the sense of "saying" and "talking" is intelligible only if it is thought in its most proper sense—as "laying" and "gathering." To name means to call forward. That which is gathered and laid down in the name, by means of such a laying, comes to light and comes to lie before us. The naming (ὄνομα), thought in terms of λέγειν, is not the expressing of a word-meaning but rather a letting-lie-before in the light wherein something stands in such a way that it has a name.

In the first place the Ἐν, the Λόγος, the destining of everything fateful, is not in its innermost essence ready to appear under the name "Zeus," i.e. to appear *as* Zeus: οὐκ ἐθέλει. Only after that does καὶ ἐθέλει follow: the Ἐν is "yet also ready."

Is it only a manner of speaking when Heraclitus says first that the Ἐν does not admit the naming in question, or does the priority of denial have its ground in the matter itself? For Ἐν Πάντα, as Λόγος, lets everything present come to presence. The Ἐν, however, is not itself one present being among others. It is in its way unique. Zeus, for his part, is not simply someone present among others. He is the highest of present beings. Thus Zeus is designated in an exceptional way in presencing; he is allotted this special designation, and appropriately called to such an apportionment (Μοῖρα) in the all-assembling Ἐν, i.e. Fate. Zeus is not himself the Ἐν, although as the one who aims lightning-bolts he executes Fate's dispensations.

That with respect to the ἐθέλει the οὐκ is designated first suggests that the Ἕν does *not* properly admit of being named Zeus, and of being thereby degraded to the level of existing as one being present among others—even if the "among" has the character of "above all other present beings."

On the other hand, according to the saying, the Ἕν does admit of being named Zeus. How? The answer is already contained in what has just been said. If the Ἕν is not apprehended as being by itself the Λόγος, if it appears rather as the Πάντα, *then* and only then does the totality of present beings show itself under the direction of the highest present being as one totality under this [unifying] One. The totality of present beings is under its highest aspect the Ἕν as Zeus. The Ἕν itself, however, as Ἕν Πάντα, is the Λόγος, the Laying that gathers. As Λόγος, the Ἕν alone is τὸ Σοφόν, the fateful as Fate itself: the gathering of destiny into presence.

If the ἀκούειν of mortals is directed to Λόγος alone, to the Laying that gathers, then mortal λέγειν is skillfully brought to the gathering of the Λόγος. Mortal λέγειν lies secured in the Λόγος. It is destined to be appropriated in ὁμολογεῖν. Thus it remains appropriated to the Λόγος. In this way mortal λέγειν is fateful. But it is never Fate itself, i.e. Ἕν Πάντα as ὁ Λόγος.

Now that the saying of Heraclitus speaks more clearly, what it says again threatens to fade into obscurity.

The Ἕν Πάντα indeed contains the clue to the way in which Λόγος in its λέγειν essentially occurs. Yet whether it is thought as "laying" or as "saying," does λέγειν forever remain merely a type of mortal behavior? If Ἕν Πάντα were the Λόγος, then would not a particular aspect of mortal being be elevated to become the fundamental trait of that which, as the destiny of presencing itself, stands above all mortal and immortal being? Does the Λόγος imply the elevation and transfer of the mortal's way-to-be to that of the unique One? Does mortal λέγειν remain only an image corresponding to the Λόγος, which is itself the Fate in which presencing as such and for all present beings rests?

Or does such questioning, which attaches itself to the guidelines of an Either-Or, not at all apply, because its approach is from the start

74

inadequate to the inquiry here undertaken? If this is so, then neither can Λόγος be the overcoming of mortal λέγειν, nor can λέγειν be simply a copying of the definitive Λόγος. Then whatever essentially occurs in the λέγειν of ὁμολογεῖν and in the λέγειν of the Λόγος has a more primordial origin—and this in the simple middle region between both. Is there a path for mortal thinking to that place?

In any case, the path remains at first confused and confounded by the very ways which early Greek thinking opened for those who were to follow. We shall limit ourselves to stepping back before the riddle, in order to get a first glimpse of several of its puzzling aspects.

The saying of Heraclitus under discussion (B 50) states, according to our translation and commentary:

Do not listen to me, the mortal speaker, but be in hearkening to the Laying that gathers; first belong to this and then you hear properly; such hearing *is* when a letting-lie-together-before occurs by which the gathering letting-lie, the Laying that gathers, lies before us as gathered; when a letting-lie of the letting-lie-before occurs, the fateful comes to pass; then the truly fateful, i.e. destiny alone, is: the unique One unifying All.

If we set aside the commentary, though not forgetting it, and try to translate into our language what Heraclitus said, his saying reads:

Attuned not to me but to the Laying that gathers: letting the Same lie: the fateful occurs (the Laying that gathers): One unifying All.

Mortals, whose essence remains appropriated in ὁμολογεῖν, are fateful when they measure the Λόγος as the Ἕν Πάντα and submit themselves to its measurement. Therefore Heraclitus says (B 43):

Ὕβριν χρὴ σβεννύναι μᾶλλον ἢ πυρκαϊήν.

Measureless pride needs to be extinguished sooner than a raging fire.

This is needed because Λόγος needs ὁμολογεῖν if present beings are to appear and shine in presencing. Ὁμολογεῖν dispatches itself without presumption into the measuring of the Λόγος.

From the saying first considered (B 50) we receive a distant counsel, which the last-named saying (B 43) indicates to be the most necessary of all:

Before you play with fire, whether it be to kindle or extinguish it, put out first the flames of presumption, which overestimates itself and takes poor measure because it forgets the essence of Λέγειν.

The translation of λέγειν as gathered-letting-lie-before, and of Λόγος as the Laying that gathers, may seem strange. Yet it is more salutary for thinking to wander into the strange than to establish itself in the obvious. Presumably Heraclitus alienated his contemporaries at least as much, although in an entirely different way, by weaving the words λέγειν and λόγος, so familiar to them, into such a saying, and by making ὁ Λόγος the guiding word of his thinking. Where does this word ὁ λόγος—which we are now attempting to think as the Laying that gathers—lead Heraclitus' thought? The word ὁ Λόγος names that which gathers all present beings into presencing and lets them lie before us in it. Ὁ Λόγος names that in which the presencing of what is present comes to pass. The presencing of present beings the Greeks call τὸ ἐόν, that is, τὸ εἶναι τῶν ὄντων, in Latin, *esse entium*. We say the Being of beings. Since the beginning of Western thought the Being of beings emerges as what is alone worthy of thought. If we think this historic development in a truly historical way, then that in which the beginning of Western thought rests first becomes manifest: that in Greek antiquity the Being of beings becomes worthy of thought *is* the beginning of the West and *is* the hidden source of its destiny. Had this beginning not safeguarded what has been, i.e. the gathering of what still endures, the Being of beings would not now govern from the essence of modern technology. Through technology the entire globe is today embraced and held fast in a kind of Being experienced in Western fashion and represented on the epistemological models of European metaphysics and science.

In the thinking of Heraclitus the Being (presencing) of beings appears as ὁ Λόγος, as the Laying that gathers. But this lightning-flash of Being remains forgotten. And this oblivion remains hidden, in its turn, because the conception of Λόγος is forthwith transformed. Thus, early on and for a long time it was inconceivable that the Being of beings could have brought itself to language in the word ὁ Λόγος.

What happens when the Being of beings, the being in its Being, the distinction between the two *as* a distinction, is brought to language? "To bring to language" usually means to express something orally or in writing. But the phrase now wishes to think something else: "to bring to language" means to secure Being in the essence of language. May we suggest that such an event prepared itself when ὁ Λόγος became the guiding word of Heraclitus' thinking, because it became the name for the Being of beings?

Ὁ Λόγος, τὸ Λέγειν, is the Laying that gathers. But at the same time λέγειν always means for the Greeks to lay before, to exhibit, to tell, to say. Ὁ Λόγος then would be the Greek name for speaking, saying, and language. Not only this. Ὁ Λόγος, thought as the Laying that gathers, would be the essence of saying [*die Sage*] as thought by the Greeks. Language would be saying. Language would be the gathering letting-lie-before of what is present in its presencing. In fact, the Greeks *dwelt* in this essential determination of language. But they never *thought* it—Heraclitus included.

The Greeks do experience saying in this way. But, Heraclitus included, they never think the essence of language expressly as the Λόγος, as the Laying that gathers.

What would have come to pass had Heraclitus—and all the Greeks after him—thought the essence of language expressly as Λόγος, as the Laying that gathers! Nothing less than this: the Greeks would have thought the essence of language from the essence of Being—indeed, as this itself. For ὁ Λόγος is the name for the Being of beings. Yet none of this came to pass. Nowhere do we find a trace of the Greeks' having thought the essence of language directly from the essence of Being. Instead, language came to be represented—indeed first of all with the Greeks—as vocalization, φωνή, as sound and voice, hence phonetically. The Greek word that corresponds to our word "language" is γλῶσσα, "tongue." Language is φωνὴ σημαντική, a vocalization which signifies something. This suggests that language attains at the outset that preponderant character which we designate with the name "expression." This correct but externally contrived representation of language, language as "expression," remains definitive from now on. It is still so today. Language is taken to be expression, and vice versa. Every kind of expression is represented as a kind of language. Art historians speak of the "language of forms." Once, however, in the beginning of Western thinking, the essence of language flashed in the light of Being—once, when Heraclitus thought the Λόγος as his guiding word, so as to think in this word the Being of beings. But the lightning abruptly vanished. No one held onto its streak of light and the nearness of what it illuminated.

We see this lightning only when we station ourselves in the storm of Being. Yet everything today betrays the fact that we bestir ourselves only to drive storms away. We organize all available means for cloud-seeding and storm dispersal in order to have calm in the face of the storm. But this calm is no tranquility. It is only anesthesia; more precisely, the narcotization of anxiety in the face of thinking.

To think is surely a peculiar affair. The word of thinkers has no authority. The word of thinkers knows no authors, in the sense of writers. The word of thinking is not picturesque; it is without charm. The word of thinking rests in the sobering quality of what it says. Just the same, thinking changes the world. It changes it in the ever darker depths of a riddle, depths which as they grow darker offer promise of a greater brightness.

The riddle has long been propounded to us in the word "Being." In this matter "Being" remains only the provisional word. Let us see to it that our thinking does not merely run after it blindly. Let us first thoughtfully consider that "Being" was originally called "presencing"—and "presencing": enduring-here-before in unconcealment.

THREE

Moira
(Parmenides VIII, 34-41)

The relation between thinking and Being animates all Western reflection. It remains the durable touchstone for determining to what extent and in what way we have been granted both the privilege and the capacity to approach that which addresses itself to historical man as to-be-thought. Parmenides names this relation in his saying (Frag. III):

> τὸ γὰρ αὐτὸ νοεῖν ἐστίν τε καὶ εἶναι.

> For thinking and Being are the same.

In another verse, Fragment VIII, he elaborates this saying. The lines read:

> ταὐτὸν δ'ἐστὶ νοεῖν τε καὶ οὕνεκεν ἔστι νόημα.
> οὐ γὰρ ἄνευ τοῦ ἐόντος, ἐν ᾧ πεφατισμένον ἐστιν,
> εὑρήσεις τὸ νοεῖν: οὐδὲν γὰρ ἢ ἔστιν ἢ ἔσται
> ἄλλο πάρεξ τοῦ ἐόντος, ἐπεὶ τό γε Μοῖρ' ἐπέδησεν
> οὖλον ἀκίνητόν τ' ἔμμεναι: τῷ πάντ' ὄνομ' ἔσται,
> ὅσσα βροτοὶ κατέθεντο πεποιθότες εἶναι ἀληθῆ,
> γίγνεσθαί τε καὶ ὄλλυσθαι, εἶναί τε καὶ οὐχί,
> καὶ τόπον ἀλλάσσειν διά τε χρόα φανὸν ἀμείβειν.

Thinking and the thought "it is" are the same. For without the being in relation to which it is uttered you cannot find thinking. For there neither is nor shall be anything outside of being, since Moira bound it to be whole and immovable. For that reason, all these will be mere names which mortals have laid down,

79

convinced that they were true: coming-to-be as well as passing away, Being as well as nonbeing, and also change of place and variation of shining colors.*

How do these eight verses more clearly bring to light the relation between thinking and Being? They seem rather to obscure it, since they themselves lead us into darkness and leave us without counsel. Let us therefore seek some sort of preliminary instruction concerning the relation between thinking and Being by pursuing the main features of previous interpretations. It has traditionally been explained in three ways, each of which we may mention briefly without showing in detail to what extent it is evidenced in the Parmenidean text. In the first, thinking is taken as something at hand, appearing alongside many other such things, and which "is" in that sense. Its being must be gauged by the standard applied to every other being of its kind, and together with those beings be aggregated into a sort of comprehensive whole. This unity of beings is called Being. Since thinking, considered as a being, is just like every other kind of being, thinking proves to be identical with Being.

One hardly needs to have recourse to philosophy in order to draw such a conclusion. The mustering of what is at hand into the totality of being seems quite natural. It involves more than thinking. Seafaring, temple building, conversation at social gatherings, every kind of human activity belongs among beings and is therefore identical with Being. One wonders why Parmenides, precisely with respect to that human activity called thinking should have insisted on expressly establishing that it is included in the realm of beings. One would certainly be justified in wondering further why Parmenides proceeds to give a special proof for this inclusion, particularly through the commonplace notion that aside from beings, and being in totality, there can be no other beings.

Rightly viewed, however, where Parmenides' doctrine is represented in such fashion one has long ceased to wonder. For by considering Parmenides' thought in this way we abandon it; it thereupon

*Cf. Diels-Kranz, *Die Fragmente der Vorsokratiker*, I, 238. Heidegger's citation of Fragment VIII differs from that of Diels-Kranz in two respects: he replaces the Greek semicolon (·) in lines 36 and 38 with a colon(:), and employs a variant spelling for ἔμεναι (1. 38). On the latter see below, p. 91—Tr.

succumbs to these crude and clumsy attempts—for which it was an effort, to be sure—to assign every being that comes to the fore, among others also thinking, a place in the totality of being.

Consequently our reflection will gain nothing by paying attention to this inept interpretation of the relationship between thinking and Being, which represents everything solely by reference to the mass of beings at hand. Still, this interpretation does give us the priceless opportunity to make the point once and for all that Parmenides nowhere explicitly says that thinking *too* is one of the many ἐόντα, one of the manifold beings, each of which at one time is and at another time is not, and therefore always brings to appearance both at once: being and nonbeing, what comes-to-be and what passes away.

In contrast to this first interpretation of Parmenides' saying—an interpretation equally accessible to everyone—another more thoughtful treatment of the text (in verses VIII, 34 ff.) at least finds "utterances difficult to understand." To assist in illuminating what is intelligible in them one has to search about for a proper guide. Where does one find it? Obviously it will be found in an understanding which has more incisively penetrated into that relation between thinking and Being which Parmenides was trying to think. Such penetration proclaims itself in a question concerning thinking or knowledge with respect to its connection with Being, i.e. with reality. The analysis of the relationship between thinking and Being, understood in this fashion, is one of the chief aims of modern philosophy. With this aim in view, philosophy has even produced a special discipline, theory of knowledge, which today in many respects serves as the chief business of philosophy. It has changed only its name, and is now called "Metaphysics" or "The Ontology of Knowledge." At present its definitive and most widespread form is being developed under the rubric of "Symbolic Logic" [*Logistik*]. Here the saying of Parmenides, by a strange and unforeseen transformation, has reached a decisive position of dominance. Thus philosophy in the modern age everywhere deems itself so situated that from its seemingly superior standpoint it can extract the true meaning from Parmenides' saying concerning the relation between thinking and Being. Considering the unchecked power of modern thinking (philosophy of existence and existentialism, along with symbolic logic, are its most effective exponents), it is necessary to emphasize more distinctly that definitive outlook within which the modern interpretation of Parmenides' fragment operates.

Modern philosophy experiences beings as objects [*Gegenstand*]. It is through and for perception that the object comes to be a "standing against." As Leibniz clearly saw, *percipere* is like an appetite which seeks out the particular being and attacks it, in order to grasp it and wholly subsume it under a concept, relating this being's presence [*Präsenz*] back to the *percipere (repraesentare). Repraesentatio*, representation [*Vorstellung*], is defined as the perceptive self-presentation (to the self as ego) of what appears.

Among the doctrines of modern philosophy there is one outstanding formulation which is unfailingly regarded as the final solution by all those who with the help of modern philosophy undertake to clarify Parmenides' saying. We mean Berkeley's proposition, which is based on the fundamental position of Descartes' metaphysics and says: *esse = percipi*, to be is at once to be represented. Being falls under the sway of representation, understood in the sense of perception. This proposition fashions the context in which the saying of Parmenides first becomes accessible to a scientific-philosophical explanation which removes it from that aura of half-poetical "presentiment" to which Presocratic thinking is usually consigned. *Esse = percipi*. Being is being represented. It is by virtue of representing that Being is. Being is identical with thinking insofar as the objectivity of objects is composed and constituted in the representing consciousness, in the "I think something." In light of this assertion regarding the relation between Being and thinking, the saying of Parmenides comes to be viewed as a crude prefiguring of contemporary doctrines of reality and the knowledge of reality.

It is no accident that Hegel, in his *Lectures on the History of Philosophy* (*Works*, 2d ed., XIII, 274), translates and discusses this saying of Parmenides concerning the relation of Being and thinking:

"Thinking, and that for the sake of which there is thought, are the same. For without the beings in which it is expressed (ἐν ᾧπεφατισμένον ἐστιν) you will not find thinking; for thinking, without beings, is and shall be nothing." This is the main thought. Thinking produces itself, and what is produced is a thought.

Thinking is thus identical with its Being; for there is nothing outside of Being, this great affirmation.

For Hegel Being is the affirmation of self-productive thought. Being is the product of thinking, of perception, in the sense in which Descartes had already interpreted *idea*. Through thinking, Being as affirmation and as the positing of representation is transposed into the realm of the "ideal." For Hegel also—though in an incomparably more thoughtful way, a way mediated by Kant—Being is the same as thinking. It is the same as thinking in that Being is what is expressed and affirmed by thinking. Thus, from the standpoint of modern philosophy, Hegel can pass the following judgment upon the saying of Parmenides:

In that this saying gives evidence of ascending into the realm of the ideal, genuine philosophizing began with Parmenides; . . . this beginning is of course still dark and indefinite and does not further explain what is contained in it; but just this explanation constitutes the development of philosophy itself—which is not yet present here. (pp. 274 ff.)

For Hegel philosophy is at hand only when the self-thinking of absolute knowledge is reality itself, and simply is. The self-perfecting elevation of Being into the thinking of Spirit as absolute reality takes place in and as speculative logic.

On the horizon of this consummation of modern philosophy Parmenides' saying appears as the very beginning of genuine philosophizing, i.e. as the beginning of logic in Hegel's sense—but only as a beginning. Parmenides' thought lacks the speculative, dialectical form which Hegel does however find in Heraclitus. Referring to Heraclitus Hegel says, "Here we see land; there is no sentence in Heraclitus which I have not taken up into my *Logic*." Hegel's *Logic* is not only the one and only suitable interpretation of Berkeley's proposition in modern times; it is its unconditioned realization. That Berkeley's assertion *esse = percipi* concerns precisely what Parmenides' saying first put into words has never been doubted. But this historical kinship of the modern proposition and the ancient saying at the same time has its proper foundation in a difference between what is said and thought in our times and what was said and thought at that time—a difference which could hardly be more decisive.

The dissimilarity between the two is so far-reaching that through it the very possibility of comprehending the difference is shattered. By indicating this difference we are at the same time giving an indication of the degree to which our own interpretation of Parmenides' saying arises from a way of thinking utterly foreign to the Hegelian approach. Does the statement *esse* = *percipi* contain the proper interpretation of the saying τὸ γὰρ αὐτὸ νοεῖν ἐστίν τε καὶ εἶναι? Do both propositions—provided we may call them propositions—say that thinking and Being are the same? And even if they do say so, do they say so in the same sense? To the attentive eye a distinction at once makes itself clear which might easily be dismissed as apparently external. In both places (Frags. III and VIII, 34-41) Parmenides words his saying so that νοεῖν (thinking) each time precedes εἶναι (Being). Berkeley, on the other hand, puts *esse* (Being) before *percipi* (thinking). This would seem to signify that Parmenides grants priority to thinking, while Berkeley grants priority to Being. Actually the situation is just the reverse: Parmenides consigns thinking to Being, while Berkeley refers Being to thinking. To correspond more adequately to the Greek saying, the modern proposition would have to run: *percipi* = *esse*.

The modern statement asserts something about Being, understood as objectivity for a thoroughgoing representation. The Greek saying assigns thinking, as an apprehending which gathers, to Being, understood as presencing. Thus every interpretation of the Greek saying that moves within the context of modern thinking goes awry from the start. Nonetheless, these multiform interpretations fulfill their inexorable function: they render Greek thinking accessible to modern representation and bolster the latter in its self-willed progression to a "higher" level of philosophy.

The first of the three viewpoints that determine all interpretations of Parmenides' saying represents thinking as something at hand and inserts it among the remaining beings. The second viewpoint, in the modern fashion, grasps Being, in the sense of the representedness of objects, as objectivity for the ego of subjectivity.

The third point of view follows one of the guidelines of ancient philosophy as determined by Plato. According to the Socratic-Platonic teaching, the Ideas endow every entity with "being," but they do not belong in the realm of αἰσθητά, the sense-perceptible. The Ideas can be purely seen only in νοεῖν, nonsensible perception. Being belongs in the realm of the νοητά, the non- and supersensible. Plotinus interprets Parmenides' saying in the Platonic sense, according to which Parmenides wants to say: Being is something nonsensible. Here the emphasis of the saying falls on thinking, although not in the way this is understood in modern philosophy. Being is identified in terms of thinking's nonsensible nature. Interpreted from the Neoplatonic perspective, Parmenides' saying is an assertion neither about thinking nor about Being, nor even about the essential belonging-together of both in their difference. The saying is rather an assertion about the equal participation of both in the realm of the nonsensible.

Each of these three viewpoints draws the early thinking of the Greeks into a region dominated by the spheres of questioning of subsequent metaphysics. Presumably, however, all later thinking which seeks dialogue with ancient thinking should listen continually from within its own standpoint, and should thereby bring the silence of ancient thinking to expression. In this process, of course, the earlier thinking is inevitably accommodated to the later dialogue, into whose frame of reference and ways of hearing it is transposed. The earlier thinking is thus, as it were, deprived of its own freedom of speech. But this accommodation in no way restricts one to an interpretation completely dedicated to reinterpreting the to-be-thought at the beginning of Western thinking exclusively in terms of subsequent modes of representation. All depends on whether the dialogue we have undertaken first of all and continually allows itself to respond to the questioning address of early thinking, or whether it simply closes itself off to such an address and cloaks early thought with the mantle of more recent doctrines. This happens as soon as subsequent thinking neglects to *inquire properly* into the ways of hearing and frames of reference of early thinking.

An effort at proper inquiry should not end in a historical investigation which merely establishes the unexpressed presuppositions underlying early thought; that is, proper inquiry is not an investigation in which these presuppositions are taken into account solely with respect to whatever subsequent interpretation either validates as already posited truth or invalidates as having been superseded by further developments. Unlike this type of investigation, proper inquiry must be a dialogue in which the ways of hearing and points of view of ancient thinking are contemplated according to their essential origin, so that the call [*Geheiss*] under which past, present, and future thinking —each in its own way—all stand, might begin to announce itself. An attempt at such inquiry should first direct its attention to the obscure passages of the ancient text, and should not settle upon those which give the appearance of easy intelligibility. To focus on the latter would end the dialogue before it has begun.

The following discussion limits itself to working through the cited text by a series of individual commentaries. These may help to prepare a thoughtful translation of early Greek speech by advancing a thinking which is awake to beginnings.

I

The topic under discussion is the relation between thinking and Being. In the first place we ought to observe that the text (VIII, 34-41) which ponders this relation more thoroughly speaks of ἐόν and not—as in Fragment III—about εἶναι. Immediately, and with some justification, one concludes from this that Fragment VIII concerns beings rather than Being. But in saying ἐόν Parmenides is in no way thinking "beings in themselves," understood as the whole to which thinking, insofar as it is some kind of entity, also belongs. Just as little does ἐόν mean εἶναι in the sense of "Being for itself," as though it were incumbent upon the thinker to set the nonsensible essential nature of Being apart from, and in opposition to, beings which are sensible. Rather ἐόν, being, is thought here in its duality as Being and beings, and is participially expressed—although the grammatical concept has not yet come explicitly into the grasp of linguistic science. This duality is at least intimated by such nuances of phrasing as "the Being *of* beings" and "beings *in* Being." In its essence, however, what unfolds is obscured more than clarified through the "in" and the "of." These expressions are far from thinking the duality as such, or from seriously questioning its unfolding.

"Being itself," so frequently invoked, is held to be true so long as it is experienced as Being, consistently understood as the Being of beings. Meanwhile the beginning of Western thinking was fated to catch an appropriate glimpse of what the word εἶναι, to be, says—in Φύσις, Λόγος, Ἕν. Since the gathering that reigns within Being unites all beings, an inevitable and continually more stubborn semblance arises from the contemplation of this gathering, namely, the illusion that Being (of beings) is not only identical with the totality of beings, but that, as identical, it is at the same time that which unifies and is even most in being [*das Seiendste*]. *For representational thinking everything comes to be a being.*

The duality of Being and beings, as something twofold, seems to melt away into nonexistence, albeit thinking, from its Greek beginnings onward, has moved within the unfolding of this duality, though without considering its situation or at all taking note of the unfolding of the twofold. What takes place at the beginning of Western thought is the unobserved decline of the duality. But this decline is not nothing. Indeed it imparts to Greek thinking the character of a beginning, in that the lighting of the Being of beings, as a lighting, is concealed. The hiddenness of this decline of the duality reigns in essentially the same way as that into which the duality itself falls. Into what does it fall? Into oblivion, whose lasting dominance conceals itself as Λήθη, to which Ἀλήθεια belongs so immediately that the former can withdraw in its favor and can relinquish to it pure disclosure in the modes of Φύσις, Λόγος, and Ἕν, as though this had no need of concealment.

But the apparently futile lighting is riddled with darkness. In it the unfolding of the twofold remains as concealed as its decline for beginning thought. However, we must be alert to the duality of Being and beings in the ἐόν in order to follow the discussion Parmenides devotes to the relation between thinking and Being.

II

Fragment III states very concisely that thinking belongs to Being. How shall we characterize this belongingness? Our question comes too late, since the laconic saying has already given the answer with its first words: τὸ γὰρ αὐτό, "For, the Same. . . ." The construction of the saying in Fragment VIII, 34 begins with the very same word: ταὐτόν. Does this word give us an answer to the question of how thinking belongs to Being, in that it says both are "the Same"? The word gives no answer. In the first place, because the determination "the Same" precludes any question about "belonging together," which can only exist between things that are different. In the second place, because the word "the Same" says nothing at all about the point of view from which, and for what reason, difference passes over into sameness. Thus τὸ αὐτό, the Same, remains the enigmatic key word for both fragments—if not for the whole of Parmenides' thought.

Of course if we are of the opinion that the word τὸ αὐτό, the Same, means "identical," and if we accept "identity" completely as the most transparent presupposition for the thinkability of whatever is thinkable, then by this opinion we become progressively more deaf to the key word, assuming that we have ever heard its call. It is sufficient, however, to keep the word in our hearing in its thought-provoking character. In doing so we remain listeners, prepared to let this enigmatic key word alone for a while in order to listen for a saying which could help us to contemplate the enigma in all its fullness.

Parmenides offers some help. In Fragment VIII he gives a clearer statement as to how we should think the "Being" to which νοεῖν belongs. Instead of εἶναι, Parmenides now says ἐόν, "being" [*das Seiend*], which enunciates the ambiguity of the duality of Being and beings. But νοεῖν calls to mind νόημα: what has been taken heed of by an attentive apprehending.

Ἐόν is explicitly identified as that οὕνεκεν ἔστι νόημα for the sake of which thankful thought comes to presence. (Concerning thinking and thanking see *What Is Called Thinking?** Part 2, Lecture 3, pp. 138 ff.)

Thinking comes to presence because of the still unspoken duality. The presencing of thinking is on the way to the duality of Being and beings. The duality presences in taking-heed-of. According to Fragment VI, taking-heed-of is already gathered to the duality by virtue of a prior λέγειν, a prior letting-lie-before. How does this come about?

*_What Is Called Thinking?_ New York, Harper & Row, 1968.—Tᴿ.

Simply through the fact that the duality on account of which mortals find themselves thinking, demands such thinking for itself.

We are still far from experiencing the duality itself—that is, at the same time, so far as it demands thinking—far from experiencing it in an essential way. Only one thing is clear from the saying of Parmenides: neither on account of ἐόντα, "beings in themselves," nor for the sake of εἶναι, "Being for itself," does thinking come to presence. That is to say: a "being in itself," does not make thinking mandatory, nor does "Being for itself" necessitate thought. Neither, taken separately, will ever let it be known to what extent "Being" calls for thinking. But because of their duality, because of the ἐόν, thinking comes to presence. The taking-heed of Being comes to presence on the way *to* the duality. In such a presencing thinking belongs to Being. What does Parmenides say about this belonging?

III

Parmenides says that νοεῖν πεφατισμένον ἐν τῷ ἐόντι. This is translated: "thinking, which as something uttered is in being." But how can we ever hope to experience and understand this being-uttered so long as we do not take the trouble to question what "utterance," "to speak," and "language" mean here, or so long as we hastily accept ἐόν as a being and let the meaning of Being remain undetermined? How can we ever come to recognize the connection of νοεῖν to πεφατισμένον so long as we do not adequately determine the νοεῖν by referring back to Fragment VI? (Cf. *What Is Called Thinking?* pp. 203 ff.) Νοεῖν, whose belonging-together with ἐόν we should like to contemplate, is grounded in and comes to presence from λέγειν. In λέγειν the letting-lie-before of what is present in its presencing occurs. Only as thus lying-before can what is present as such admit the νοεῖν, the taking-heed-of. Accordingly, the νόημα as νοούμενον of the νοεῖν is already a λεγόμενον of the λέγειν. In the Greek experience, the essence of saying rests in λέγειν. On that account νοεῖν is essentially—not peripherally or accidentally—something said. Certainly not everything said need be an utterance. It can also, and sometimes must, be a silence. Every utterance and every silence is already something said, though the reverse does not always hold.

In what does the difference between something said and something uttered consist? For what reason does Parmenides characterize the νοούμενον and νοεῖν (VIII, 34 ff.) as πεφατισμένον? This word is correctly translated in dictionaries as "utterance." But how are we to experience an uttering which gets its name from φάσκειν and φάναι? Does "utterance" here merely stand for the vocalization (φωνή) of what a word or sentence signifies (σημαίνειν)? Is speaking out, uttering, to be grasped here as the expression of something interior (something psychical), and so divided into two component parts—the phonetic and the semantic? There is no trace of this to be found in the experience of speaking as φάναι, the experience of speech as φάσις. Φάσκειν implies "to invoke," "to name with praise," "to call upon," all of which depend upon the fact that the verb has its essence in letting something appear. Φάσμα is the shining of the stars and of the moon, it is their way of coming forward into view and of self-concealing. Φάσεις means "phases." The changing forms of the moon's shining are its phases. Φάσις is the saying; to say means to bring forward into view. Φημί, "I say," has the same (though not identical) essence as λέγω: to bring what is present in its presencing forward into shining appearance, into lying-before.

Parmenides thus wishes to discuss where νοεῖν belongs. For only where it belongs and is at home can we find it; only there can we experience through our findings how far thinking belongs with Being. If Parmenides experiences νοεῖν as πεφατιομένον, this does not mean that he experiences it as an "utterance" which is to be discovered in spoken conversation or in written characters, i.e. in some sort of sensibly perceptible entities. We would miss the mark entirely, putting the greatest possible distance between ourselves and Greek thinking, if we accepted this notion, and if we further desired to represent both speaking and what is spoken as "conscious experiences," and to establish thinking within the confines of these experiences as an act of consciousness. Νοεῖν, taking-heed-of, and what it takes up, are something said, something brought forward into view. But where? Parmenides says: ἐν τῷ ἐόντι, in ἐόν, in the duality of presencing and what is present. This gives us food for thought and thoroughly frees us from the hasty presupposition that thinking is something expressed in an utterance: there is nowhere any suggestion of that.

To what extent can and must voεῖν, thinking, come to light in the duality? To the extent that the unfolding in the duality of presencing and present beings invokes λέγειν, letting-lie-before, and with the released letting-lie of what lies before us, grants voεῖν something it can take heed of and thus preserve. But Parmenides does not yet think the duality as such; he does not at all think through the unfolding of the twofold. He does, however, say (Frag. VIII, 35 ff.): οὐ γὰρ ἄνευ τοῦ ἐόντος . . . εὑρήσεις τὸ νοεῖν. "For you cannot find thinking apart from the duality." Why not? Because thinking belongs with ἐόν in the gathering that ἐόν calls for; and because thinking itself, resting in the λέγειν, completes the gathering called for, thus responding to its belonging to ἐόν as a belonging which ἐόν uses. For voεῖν takes up, not just anything at random, but only that One designated in Fragment VI: ἐόν ἔμμεναι,* whatever is present in its presencing.

Insofar as what is thought-provoking, though not yet thought, is announced in Parmenides' exposition, so far does the fundamental requirement clearly come to light for proper reflection upon Parmenides' statement that thinking belongs to Being. We have to learn to think the essence of language from the saying, and to think saying as letting-lie-before (λόγος) and as bringing-forward-into-view (φάσις). To satisfy this demand remains a difficult task because that first illumination of the essence of language as saying disappears immediately into a veiling darkness and yields ascendancy to a characterization of language which relentlessly represents it in terms of φωνή, vocalization—a system of signs and significations, and ultimately of data and information.

---

*In the Ionian dialect and in epic usage the verb εἶναι (to be) may appear either as ἔμεναι or ἔμμεναι. In his commentary on Aristotle's *Physics* Simplicius, for no apparent reason, ascribes both forms to Parmenides. The first variant appears at 144, 29 (Diels-Kranz VIII, 38), the second at 117, 2 (Diels-Kranz VI, 1). Heidegger reproduces the second variant (ἔμμεναι, DK VI, 1) throughout. With a shift of accent to the penult this second form becomes ἔμμεναι, an Attic isomorph—used also by Herodotus, however—which means to dwell in or abide by; or of things, to remain fixed, stand fast.—TR.

IV

Even now, when the way in which thinking belongs to Being has been brought somewhat more clearly to light, we are scarcely able to hear the enigmatic key word of the saying—τὸ αὐτό, the Same—in its enigmatic fullness. But when we see that the duality of the ἐόν, the presencing of what is present, gathers thinking to itself, then the governing duality gives us a clue to the profound riddle of what is hidden by the ordinarily empty and insignificant word "the Same."

Is it from the *unfolding* of the twofold that the duality in turn calls thinking onto the path of "for its own sake," thereby requiring also the belonging-together of the presencing (of what is present) and thinking? But what is the unfolding of the twofold? How does it happen? Do we find any basis in Parmenides' saying for a proper inquiry into the unfolding of the duality, or for hearing what is essential to the unfolding in what the enigmatic key word of the saying silently conceals? We find nothing immediate.

Still, it should occur to us that in both forms of the saying concerning the relation of thinking and Being the enigmatic key word stands at the beginning. Fragment III says, "For the Same is taking-heed-of and so too presencing (of what is present)." Fragment VIII, 34, says, "The Same is taking-heed-of and (that) toward which heedful perception is on the way." What does situating the word at the beginning signify in what this passage says? What tone is Parmenides trying to set in letting us hear this resounding emphasis? Ostensibly the dominant tone. In it resounds the anticipation of *what* the saying really has to say. Grammatically, what it says is called the predicate of the sentence. Thus the subject here would be νοεῖν (thinking) in its connection with εἶναι (Being). In accordance with the Greek text this is the sense in which one must interpret the grammatical structure of the saying. By placing its enigmatic key word at the beginning as predicate, the saying calls on us to dwell on the word attentively, returning to it again and again. But even so, the word says nothing about what we would like to learn.

Therefore we are compelled to focus our gaze relentlessly upon the preferred position of τὸ αὐτό, the Same, and to make a daring attempt to think from the duality of ἐόν (the presencing of what is present) to its unfolding. We are aided in our purpose by the insight that thinking, when brought forward into view within the duality of the ἐόν, is something said therein, πεφατισμένον.

As a result, what reigns in the duality is φάσις, saying as the invocative and insistent bringing-forward-into-view. What does the saying bring to appear? The presencing of what is present. The saying that comes to pass and governs in the duality is the gathering of presencing, in whose shining what is present can appear. What Parmenides thinks as Φάσις Heraclitus calls the Λόγος, the letting-lie-before that gathers.

What happens in Φάσις and in Λόγος? Could the gathering-calling saying which reigns in them be that bringing which brings forth a shining? Which gives the lighting in whose endurance presencing is first illuminated, so that in its light what is present appears, thus governing the duality of both? Could the unfolding of the twofold consist in this, that a shining which illuminates itself comes to pass? The Greeks experience its basic character as disclosure [*Entbergen*]. Correspondingly, disclosure reigns in the unfolding of the twofold. The Greeks call it 'Αλήθεια.

If indeed Parmenides was saying something about 'Αλήθεια, he must have been thinking within the unfolding of the twofold. Does he mention 'Αλήθεια? Of course he does, right at the beginning of his "Didactic Poem." Even more: 'Αλήθεια is the goddess. Listening to what she says, Parmenides speaks his own thought—although he leaves unsaid what the essence of 'Αλήθεια might be rooted in. He also leaves unthought in what sense of divinity 'Αλήθεια is a goddess. All this remains for the early thinking of the Greeks as obviously outside the realm of the thought-provoking as any explanation of the enigmatic key word, τὸ αὐτό, the Same.

Presumably, however, there is some hidden link connecting all these unthought elements. The introductory lines of the poem (I, 22 ff.) are not poetical finery masking an abstract conceptual work. We make the dialogue with Parmenides' way of thinking too easy if we ignore the mythic experience in the philosopher's words, and then object that the goddess 'Αλήθεια is an extremely vague and empty mental construct in comparison with the sharply delineated "divine persons," Hera, Athene, Demeter, Aphrodite, and Artemis. Such objections are advanced as if we already possessed old and reliable knowledge about the divinity of the Greek gods—as if we were certain that it makes sense here to talk about "persons," and as if it had long been determined that if the essence of truth should appear as a goddess it could do so only as the abstract personification of a concept. Thought has scarcely touched upon the essence of the mythical, especially with regard to the fact that the μῦθος is the saying, while saying is the calling bringing-into-appearance. Consequently we would be better advised to continue questioning with caution, while listening to what is said:

καί με Θεὰ πρόφρων ὑπεδέξατο, χεῖρα δε χειρί
δεξιτερὴν ἕλεν, ὧδε δ' ἔπος φάτο καί με προσηύδα:

And the goddess received me with thoughtful
affection, as hand with hand
she took my right and so gave voice and sang
to me:

What is herewith given the thinker to think remains at the same time veiled with respect to its essential origins. This affirms rather than denies that disclosure rules in what the thinker says, and rules as what the thinker heeds, since this points the way into what is to-be-thought. But what is to-be-thought is named in the enigmatic key word τὸ αὐτό, the Same. What is so named expresses the relation of thinking to Being.

For that reason we must at least ask whether or not the unfolding of the twofold, taken specifically as the disclosure of the presencing of what is present, is tacitly contained in the αὐτό, the Same. When we presume that such is the case we do not advance beyond the thought of Parmenides; rather, we only reach back into what must be thought even more primordially.

A discussion of the saying that bears on the relation of thinking and Being inevitably succumbs to the appearance of being arbitrary and forced.

The construction of the passage τὸ γὰρ αὐτὸ νοεῖν ἐστίν τε καὶ εἶναι, grammatically represented, now shows itself in a different light. The enigmatic key word, τὸ αὐτό, the Same, with which the saying begins, is no longer a predicate repositioned to stand first, but rather the subject—what lies at the core, what supports and maintains. The inconspicuous ἐστίν, "is," now means "comes to presence," "endures," and further, the bestowal of what endures. As such, τὸ αὐτό, the Same reigns. Specifically, it reigns as the unfolding of the twofold—an unfolding in the sense of disclosure. That which unfolds, and in unfolding reveals the twofold, allows taking-heed-of to get under way toward the gathering perception of the presencing of what is present. Truth, characterized as the disclosure of the duality, lets thinking, from out of this duality, belong to Being. What is silently concealed in the enigmatic key word τὸ αὐτό is the revealing bestowal of the belonging-together of the duality and the thinking that comes forward into view within it.

V

Thus thinking does not belong together with Being because it is *also* something present and therefore to be counted in the totality of presencing—which means here the whole of what is present. Admittedly, it seems as though Parmenides represents the connection between thinking and Being in just this fashion. But he offers some justification, tacking it on by means of a γάρ (for). His explanation states (VIII, 36 ff.), πάρεξ τοῦ ἐόντος: outside of beings there was, is, and will be nothing else in being (following Bergk's conjecture, οὐδ' ἦν). However, τὸ ἐόν does not say "beings," but rather names the duality. Naturally there is never a presencing of what is present outside it, since presencing as such is grounded in, appears in, and shines out of the unfolded light of the twofold.

But why does Parmenides expressly append this explanation with regard to the relation of thinking to Being? Because the name νοεῖν, "thinking," in not sounding the same as εἶναι, gives the appearance of actually being an ἄλλο, something different, something set opposite Being and therefore apart from it. But not only does the pronunciation of the name appear to maintain itself "alongside" and "apart from" ἐόν, but also what the name names. This appearance is no mere illusion. For λέγειν and νοεῖν let what is present lie before us in the light of presencing. Accordingly, they themselves lie opposite presencing, though certainly not as two independently existing objects. The conjunction of λέγειν and νοεῖν (according to Fragment VI) liberates the ἐὸν ἔμμεναι, presencing in its appearance, for perception, and therefore does in a certain sense hold itself apart from ἐόν. In one respect thinking is outside the duality toward which it makes its way, required by and responding to it. In another respect, this very "making its way toward . . ." remains within the duality, which is never simply an indifferently represented distinction between Being and beings, but rather comes to presence from the revealing unfolding. It is this unfolding that, as 'Αλήθεια, bestows on every presencing the light in which something present can appear.

But disclosure, while it bestows the lighting of presencing, at the same time needs a letting-lie-before and a taking-up-into-perception if what is present is to appear, and by this need binds thinking to its belonging-together with the duality. Therefore by no means is there somewhere and somehow something present outside the duality.

This entire discussion would be something arbitrarily spun out in thought and insinuated by hindsight had not Parmenides himself explained why anything outside of presencing, anything besides the ἐόν, is impossible.

VI

Considered grammatically, what the thinker says here about the ἐόν stands in a subordinate clause. Anyone who has only minimal experience in hearing what great thinkers say will probably pause to ponder the strange fact that they say what is to be thought in a casually attached dependent clause and let it go at that. The play of the calling, brightening, expanding light is not actually visible. It shines imperceptibly, like morning light upon the quiet splendor of lilies in a field or roses in a garden.

Parmenides' subordinate clause—in reality his "sentence of sentences"—runs (VIII, 37 ff.):

. . . ἐπεὶ τό γε Μοῖρ' ἐπέδησεν οὖλον ἀκίνητόν τ' ἔμμεναι:

. . . since Moira bound it (being) to be a whole and immovable.

(W. Kranz)

Parmenides speaks of ἐόν, of the presencing (of what is present), and of duality, and in no sense of "beings." He names the Μοῖρα, the apportionment, which allots by bestowing and so unfolds the twofold. The apportionment dispenses [*beschickt*], (provides and presents) through the duality. Apportionment is the dispensation of presencing, as the presencing of what is present, which is gathered in itself and therefore unfolds of itself. Μοῖρα is the destining of "Being," in the sense of ἐόν. Μοῖρα has dispensed the destiny of Being, τό γε, into the duality, and thus has bound it to totality and immobility, from which and in which the presencing of what is present comes to pass.

In the destining of duality, however, only presencing attains a shining, and only what is present attains appearance. Destiny altogether conceals both the duality as such and its unfolding. The essence of 'Αλήθεια remains veiled. The visibility it bestows allows the presencing of what is present to arise as outer appearance [*Aussehen*], (εἶδος) and aspect [*Gesicht*], (ἰδέα). Consequently the perceptual relation to the presencing of what is present is defined as "seeing" (εἰδέναι). Stamped with this character of *visio*, knowledge and the evidence of knowledge cannot renounce their essential derivation from luminous disclosure, even where truth has been transformed into the certainty of self-consciousness. *Lumen naturale,* natural light, i.e. the illumination of reason, already presupposes the disclosure of the duality. The same holds true of the Augustinian and medieval views of light—not to mention their Platonic origins—which could only develop under the tutelage of an 'Αλήθεια already reigning in the destiny of the duality.

If we wish to speak of the history of Being we must first have considered that Being says: presencing of what is present: duality. Only on the basis of Being, so considered, can we first ask with adequate thoughtfulness what "history" might mean here. History is the destining of the duality. It is the revealing, unfolding bestowal of luminous presencing in which what is present appears. The history of Being is never a sequence of events which Being traverses for itself. It is certainly not an "object" which might offer new possibilities of historical representation, willing to put itself in the place of prior observations of the history of metaphysics with the presumption of knowing better than they.

What Parmenides in his inconspicuous subordinate clause says about Μοῖρα, into whose grasp ἐόν has been released as the duality, reveals to the thinker the breadth of vision fatefully reserved for the path he treads. For in this expanse appears that in which the presencing (of what is present) manifests itself: τὰ σήματα τοῦ ἐόντος. There are many (πολλά) of these σήματα. They are not signposts for something else. They are the manifold shining of presencing itself, out of the unfolded duality.

VII

But we have not yet exhaustively recounted what it is that Μοῖρα in its dispensing metes out. Therefore an essential feature of the nature of its governance still remains unthought. What is the significance of the fact that destiny releases the presencing of what is present into the duality, and so binds it to wholeness and rest?

To take proper measure of what Parmenides says about this problem in the lines that follow his subordinate clause (VIII, 39 ff.), it is necessary to recollect something previously mentioned (III). The unfolding of the twofold reigns as φάσις, saying as bringing-forward-into-view. The duality conceals within itself both νοεῖν *and* its thought (νόημα) as something said. What is taken up in thinking, however, is the presencing of what is present. The thoughtful saying that corresponds to the duality is the λέγειν, the letting-lie-before of presencing. It occurs, and occurs only, on the thought-path of the thinker who has been called by 'Αλήθεια.

But what becomes of the φάσις (saying) reigning in revealing destiny if this destiny should abandon what is unfolded in the twofold to the everyday perception of mortals? Mortals accept (δέχεσθαι, δόξα) whatever is immediately, abruptly, and first of all offered to them. They never concern themselves about preparing a path of thought. They never really hear the call of the disclosure of the duality. They keep to what is unfolded in the twofold, and only to that aspect which immediately makes a claim upon mortals; that is, they keep to what is present without considering presencing. They relinquish all their affairs to what is commonly assumed, τὰ δοκοῦντα (Frag. I, 31). They take this to be what is unconcealed, ἀληθῆ (VIII, 39), for it really does appear to them and is thus something revealed. But what becomes of their speech if it is not capable of being a λέγειν, a letting-lie-before? The ordinary speech of mortals, insofar as they do not consider presencing, that is, insofar as they do not think, ends up as a speaking of names in which vocalization and the immediately perceptible form of the word, as spoken or written, are stressed.

The unequivocal restriction of speech (of letting-lie-before) to word-signs shatters the gathering taking-heed-of. The latter now becomes κατατίθεσθαι (VIII, 39), establishing, which simply secures this or that as a hasty opinion. Everything so secured remains ὄνομα. Parmenides is in no way saying that what is ordinarily assumed becomes a "mere" name. But what is thus assumed is given over to a speaking entirely guided by current terms which, rashly spoken, say everything about everything and wander aimlessly in the ". . . as well as. . . ."

Perception of what is present (of ἐόντα) also names εἶναι and knows presencing, although it knows nonpresencing just as fleetingly; of course, it does not know this in the same way as does thinking, which for its part is concerned with what is withheld from the duality (the μὴ ἐόν). Ordinary opinion knowₔ only εἶναί τε καὶ οὐχί (VIII, 40), presencing as well as nonpresencing. The stress in this knowing falls on the τε–καί, the "as well as." And where ordinary perception, speaking in words, encounters rise and fall, it is satisfied with the "as well as" of coming-to-be, γίγνεσθαι [*Entstehen*], and passing away, ὄλλυσθαι [*Vergehen*]. It never perceives place, τόπος, as an abode, as what the twofold offers as a home to the presencing of what is present. In the "as well as," the ordinary opinion of mortals merely follows the "here and there" (ἀλλάσσειν, VIII, 41) of particular "places." Ordinary perception certainly moves within the lightedness of what is present and sees what is shining out, φανόν (VIII, 41), in color; but is dazzled by changes of color, ἀμείβειν, and pays no attention to the still light of the lighting that emanates from duality and is Φάσις: the bringing-forward-into-view—the way the word speaks, not the way in which terms as mere names speak.

Τῷ πάντ᾽ ὄνομ᾽ ἔσται (VIII, 38): thereby will everything (that is present) become present in a merely presumed disclosure which permits the predominance of terms. How does this happen? Through Μοῖρα, through the destining of the disclosure of the duality. How are we to understand this? In the unfolding of the twofold what is present comes to appear with the shining of presencing. What is present is itself also something said, but said in name-words, in whose speaking the ordinary speech of mortals moves. The destining of the disclosure of the duality (of ἐόν) yields what is present (τὰ ἐόντα) to the everyday perception of mortals.

How does this fateful yielding occur? Already only insofar as the twofold as such, and therefore its unfolding, remain hidden. But then does self-concealment reign at the heart of disclosure? A bold thought. Heraclitus thought it. Parmenides unwittingly experienced this thought insofar as he heard the call of ᾽Αλήθεια and contemplated the Μοῖρα of ἐόν, the destining of the duality, with a view to what is present and also to presencing.

Parmenides would not have been a thinker at the earliest dawn of that thinking which is sent into the destiny of the duality if he had not thought within the area of the riddle which is silently contained in the enigmatic key word τὸ αὐτό, the Same. Herein is concealed what is thought-worthy, what in the very predominance of what is present (τὰ ἐόντα, τὰ δοκοῦντα) gives us food for thought: as the relation of thinking to Being, as the truth of Being in the sense of the disclosure of the duality, and as withholding from the twofold (μὴ ἐόν).

The dialogue with Parmenides never comes to an end, not only because so much in the preserved fragments of his "Didactic Poem" still remains obscure, but also because what is said there continually deserves more thought. This unending dialogue is no failing. It is a sign of the boundlessness which, in and for remembrance, nourishes the possibility of a transformation of destiny.

But anyone who only expects thinking to give assurances, and awaits the day when we can go beyond it as unnecessary, is demanding that thought annihilate itself. That demand appears in a strange light if we consider that the essence of mortals calls upon them to heed a call which beckons them toward death. As the outermost possibility of mortal *Dasein,* death is not the end of the possible but the highest keeping (the gathering sheltering) of the mystery of calling disclosure.

FOUR

Aletheia
(Heraclitus, Fragment B 16)

———✦———

He is called "the Obscure," ὁ Σκοτεινός. Heraclitus had this reputation even when his writings were preserved intact. Today we know only fragments of his work. Later thinkers—Plato and Aristotle; subsequent authors and philosophical scholars—Theophrastus, Sextus Empiricus, Diogenes Laertius, and Plutarch; even Church Fathers—Hippolytus, Clement of Alexandria, and Origen—all cite passages from Heraclitus here and there in their own works. Thanks to research in philology and history of philosophy, these quotations have been collected as fragments. Sometimes the fragments comprise several sentences, sometimes only one sentence, and occasionally they consist of mere phrases or isolated words.

The train of thought of these later thinkers and writers determines their selection and arrangement of Heraclitus' words. This in turn delimits the space available for any interpretation of them. Thus a closer examination of their place of origin in the writings of subsequent authors yields only the context into which the quotation has been placed, not the Heraclitean context from which it was taken. The quotations and the sources, taken together, still do not yield what is essential: the definitive, all-articulating unity of the inner structure of Heraclitus' writing. Only a constantly advancing insight into this structure will reveal the point from which the individual fragments are speaking, and in what sense each of them, as a saying, must be heard. Because we can scarcely surmise what the well-spring is that gives the writing of Heraclitus its unity, and because we find this source so difficult to think, we are justified in calling this thinker "the Obscure." Even the inherent meaning of what this epithet says to us remains obscure.

Heraclitus is called "the Obscure." But he is the Lucid. For he tells of the lighting whose shining he attempts to call forth into the language of thinking. Insofar as it illuminates, the lighting endures. We call its illumination the lighting [*die Lichtung*]. What belongs to it, and how and where it takes place, still remain to be considered. The word "light" means lustrous, beaming, brightening. Lighting bestows the shining, opens what shines to an appearance. The open is the realm of unconcealment and is governed by disclosure. What belongs to the latter, and whether and to what extent disclosing and lighting are the Same, remain to be asked.

An appeal to the meaning of ἀληθεσία accomplishes nothing, and will never produce anything useful.* Further, we must ask whether what is entertained under the rubrics "truth," "certainty," "objectivity," and "reality" has the slightest bearing upon the direction in which revealing and lighting point thought. Presumably, the thinking that goes in such a direction has more at stake than a securing of objective truth—in the sense of valid propositions. Why is it that we are ever and again so quick to forget the subjectivity that belongs to every objectivity? How does it happen that even when we do note that they belong together, we still try to explain each from the standpoint of the other, or introduce some third element which is supposed to embrace both subject and object? Why is it that we stubbornly resist considering even once whether the belonging-together of subject and object does not arise from something that first imparts their nature to both the object and its objectivity, and the subject and its subjectivity, and hence is prior to the realm of their reciprocity? That our thinking finds it so toilsome to be in this bestowal, or even on the lookout for it, cannot be blamed on a narrowness of contemporary intellect or resis-

---

*Although Heidegger positively discourages us from doing so, we offer the following philogical information: ἀληθεσία is a substantive form constructed from ἀληθής (–ές), an adjectival form of ἀλήθεια. T. Gaisford's *Etymologicum Magnum* (Oxford, 1848), pp. 62, 51, discusses it as follows: λήθω = λανθάνω: ἀληθὲς τὸ μὴ λήθη ὑποπτίον. Λήθω is a collateral form of λανθάνω, I escape notice, am hidden, unseen or forgotten by others. Gaisford describes ἀληθές as that which does not sink into λήθη, the source of oblivion. Liddell-Scott translate ἀληθές as "unconcealed." Hence ἀληθεσία might be rendered as "unconcealment."—TR.

tance to unsettling or disruptive views. Rather we may surmise something else: that we know too much and believe too readily ever to feel at home in a questioning which is powerfully experienced. For that we need the ability to wonder at what is simple, and to take up that wonder as our abode.

Of course, "simple" assertion and repetition that the literal meaning of ἀληθεσία is "unconcealment" will not give us what is simple. Unconcealment is the chief characteristic of that which has already come forward into appearance and has left concealment behind. That is the significance here of the a–, which only came to be classified as the alpha-privative by a grammar based upon later Greek thought. The connection with λήθη, concealment, and concealment itself do not diminish in importance for our thinking simply because the unconcealed is immediately experienced only as what has come forward in appearance, or what is present.

Wonder first *begins* with the question, "What does all this mean and how could it happen?" How can we arrive at such a beginning? Perhaps by abandoning ourselves to a wonder which is on the lookout for what we call lighting and unconcealing?

Thoughtful wonder speaks in questioning. Heraclitus says:

τὸ μὴ δῦνόν ποτε πῶς ἄν τις λάθοι;

How can one hide himself before that which never sets?
(Diels-Kranz)

The saying is numbered as Fragment 16. But because of its inner significance and ultimate implications, perhaps we ought to consider it the *first*. Heraclitus' saying is quoted by Clement of Alexandria in his *Paidagogos* (Bk. III, chap. 10) to support a theological-educational position. He writes:

λήσεται [!] μὲν γὰρ ἴσως τὸ αἰσθητὸν φῶς τις, τὸ δὲ νοητὸν ἀδύνατόν ἐστιν, ἢ ὥς φησιν Ἡράκλειτος. . . .

"Perhaps one can hide from the light perceived by the senses, but it is impossible to do so before spiritual light, as Heraclitus says. . . ." Clement is thinking about the ever-present God who sees everything, even the sin committed in darkness. Thus his work *The Teacher* says in another place (Bk. III, chap. 5): οὕτως γὰρ μόνως ἀπτώς τις διαμένει, εἰ πάντοτε συμπαρεῖναι νομίζοι τὸν θεόν. "In this way alone will a man never fall, if he hold to the belief that God is everywhere present with him." Who would gainsay the fact that Clement, pursuing his theologico-pedagogic intentions, put the words of Heraclitus—seven centuries later—into a Christian frame of reference, thereby imposing his own interpretation on them? The Church Father was thinking about sinners hiding themselves from the light. Heraclitus, on the other hand, speaks only about "remaining concealed." Clement means the supersensible Light, τὸν θεόν, God, the God of Christian faith. Heraclitus, however, mentions only the never-setting. Whether or not this "only"—emphasized by us—signifies a limitation or something else is now, and will in what follows remain, an open question.

What advantage would there be in arguing that this theological interpretation of the fragment is simply incorrect? At best, such an argument could leave the impression that the following remarks cherish the notion that they engage Heraclitus in the one absolutely correct way. Our task limits itself to getting closer to the words of the Heraclitean saying. This could help to bring some future thinking within range of still unheard intimations.

Since these proceed from the call under which thinking stands, there is little to be gained from comparing thinkers and calculating their proximity to these intimations. Rather, all our efforts should be directed toward bringing ourselves closer to the realm of what is to be thought by means of a dialogue with an early thinker.

Discerning minds understand that Heraclitus speaks in one way to Plato, in another to Aristotle, in another to a Church Father, and in others to Hegel and to Nietzsche. If one remains embroiled in a historical grasp of these various interpretations, then one has to view each of them as only relatively correct. Such a multiplicity necessarily threatens us with the specter of relativism. Why? Because the historical ledger of interpretations has already expunged any questioning dialogue with the thinker—it probably never entered such dialogue in the first place.

The respective difference of each dialogical interpretation of thought is a sign of an unspoken fullness to which even Heraclitus himself could only speak by following the path of the insights afforded *him.* Wishing to pursue the "objectively correct" teaching of Heraclitus means refusing to run the salutary risk of being confounded by the truth of a thinking.

The following remarks lead to no conclusions. They point toward the event [*das Ereignis*].

Heraclitus' saying is a question. The word with which the fragment ends—"end" understood as τέλος—names that from which the questioning begins. It is the domain in which thinking moves. The word into which the question ascends is λάθοι. What could be easier to establish than this: that λανθάνω, aorist ἔλαθον, means "I am hidden"? Nonetheless, we are scarcely capable of immediately rediscovering just how this word speaks in Greek.

Homer (*Odyssey,* VIII, 83 ff.) tells how Odysseus, in the Phaeacian king's palace, covered his head each time at the minstrel Demodocus' song, whether happy or sad, and thus hidden from those present, wept. Verse 93 runs: ἔνθ᾽ ἄλλους μὲν πάντας ἐλάνθανε δάκρυα λείβων. Consistent with the spirit of our own language, we translate: "Then he shed tears, without all the others noticing it." The German translation by Voss comes closer to what the Greek says, since it carries the important verb ἐλάνθανε over into the German formulation: "He concealed his flowing tears from all the other guests." Ἐλάνθανε, however, does not mean the transitive "he concealed," but "he remained concealed"—as the one who was shedding tears. "Remaining concealed" is the key word in the Greek. German, on the other hand, says: he wept, without the others noticing it. Correspondingly, we translate the well-known Epicurean admonition λάθε βιώσας as "Live in hiding." Thought from a Greek perspective, this saying means: "As the one who leads his life, remain concealed (therein)." Concealment here defines the way in which a man should be present among others. By the manner of its saying, the Greek announces that concealing— and therefore at the same time remaining unconcealed—exercises a commanding preeminence over every other way in which what is present comes to presence. The fundamental trait of presencing itself is determined by remaining concealed and unconcealed. One need not begin with a seemingly capricious etymology of ἀλήθεσία in order to experience how universally the presencing of what is present comes to language only in shining, self-manifesting, lying-before, arising, bringing-itself-before, and in assuming an outward appearance.

All this, in its undisturbed harmony, would be unthinkable within Greek existence and language if remaining-concealed/remaining-unconcealed did not hold sway as that which really has no need to bring itself expressly to language, since this language itself arises from it.

Accordingly, the Greek experience in the case of Odysseus does not proceed from the premise that the guests present are represented as subjects who in their subjective behavior fail to grasp weeping Odysseus as an object of their perception. On the contrary, what governs the Greek experience is a concealment surrounding the one in tears, a concealment which isolates him from the others. Homer does not say: Odysseus concealed his tears. Nor does the poet say: Odysseus concealed himself as one weeping. Rather, he says: Odysseus remained concealed. We must ponder this matter ever more strenuously, even at the risk of becoming diffuse and fastidious. A lack of sufficient insight into this problem will mean, for us, that Plato's interpretation of presencing as ἰδέα remains either arbitrary or accidental.

A few verses before the one we have cited, Homer says (1. 86): αἴδετο γὰρ Φαίηκας ὑπ' ὀφρύσι δάκρυα λείβων. In keeping with idiomatic German Voss translates: (Odysseus covered his head) "so that the Phaeacians could not see his wet lashes." Voss in fact leaves the key word untranslated: αἴδετο. Odysseus shied away—as one shedding tears before the Phaeacians. But doesn't this quite clearly mean the same as: he hid himself before the Phaeacians out of a sense of shame? Or must we also think shying away, αἰδώς, from remaining-concealed, granted that we are striving to get closer to its essence as the Greeks experienced it? Then "to shy away," would mean to withdraw and remain concealed in reluctance or restraint *(Verhoffen)*, keeping to oneself.

Typically Greek, this poetic vision of Odysseus weeping beneath his cloak makes clear how the poet feels the governance of presencing—a meaning of Being which, though still unthought, has already become destiny. Presencing is luminous self-concealing. Shying away corresponds to it. It is a reserved remaining-concealed before the closeness of what is present. It is the sheltering of what is present within the intangible nearness of what remains in coming—that coming which is an increasing self-veiling. Thus shying-away, and everything related to it, must be thought in the brilliant light of remaining-concealed.

Consequently, we must also be prepared to consider more thoughtfully another Greek word, whose stem is λαθ–. This is ἐπιλανθάνεσθαι. The correct translation is "to forget." On the basis of this lexical correctness everything seems perfectly clear. We act as if forgetting were the most transparent thing in the world. Only fleetingly does anyone notice that there is a reference to "remaining concealed" in the corresponding Greek word.

But what does "forgetting" mean? Modern man, who puts all his stock into forgetting as quickly as possible, certainly ought to know what it is. But he does not. He has forgotten the essence of forgetting, assuming he ever thought about it fully, i.e. thought it out within the essential sphere of oblivion. The continuing indifference toward the essence of forgetting does not result simply from the superficiality of our contemporary way of life. What takes place in such indifference comes from the essence of oblivion itself. It is inherent in it to withdraw itself and to founder in the wake of its own concealment. The Greeks experienced oblivion, λήθη, as a destining of concealment.

Λανθάνομαι says: I am—with respect to my relation to something usually unconcealed—concealed from myself. The unconcealed, for its own part, is thereby concealed—even as I am concealed from myself in relation to it. What is present subsides into concealment in such a way that I, because of this concealing, remain concealed from myself as the one from whom what is present withdraws. At the same time, this very concealing is itself thereby concealed. That is what takes place in the occurrence to which we refer when we say: I have forgotten (something). When we forget, something doesn't just slip away from us. Forgetting itself slips into a concealing, and indeed in such a way that we ourselves, along with our relation to what is forgotten, fall into concealment. The Greeks, therefore, speaking in the middle voice, intensify it: ἐπιλανθάνομαι. Thus they also identify the concealment into which man falls by reference to its relation to what is withdrawn from him by concealment.

Both in the way the Greek employs λανθάνειν, to remain concealed, as a basic and predominant verb, as well as in the experience of the forgetting of remaining-concealed, this much is made sufficiently clear: λανθάνω, I remain concealed, does not signify just a form of human behavior among many others, but identifies the basic trait of every response to what is present or absent—if not, indeed, the basic trait of presence and absence themselves.

Now, if this word λήθω, I remain concealed, speaks to us in the saying of a thinker, and if perhaps it concludes a thoughtful question, then we are bound to ponder the word and what it says as comprehensively and as persistently as we can today.

Every remaining-concealed includes a relation to the sort of thing from which the concealed has withdrawn, but toward which in many cases it remains directly inclined. The Greek names in the accusative that to which what has withdrawn into concealment remains related: ἐνθ᾽ ἄλλους μὲν πάντας ἐλάνθανε. . . .

Heraclitus asks: πῶς ἄν τις λάθοι—"how could anyone remain concealed?" Relative to what? To what is named in the preceding words, with which the fragment begins: τὸ μὴ δῦνόν ποτε, that which never sets. The "anyone" mentioned here is consequently not the subject in relation to which something else remains concealed, but the "anyone" who comes into question with respect to the possibility of *his own* remaining-concealed. Heraclitus' question is not first and foremost a consideration of concealment and unconcealment with regard to the sort of men whom we, with our modern habits of representation, like to interpret as carriers—or even creators—of unconcealment. Heraclitus' question, expressed in modern terms, thinks the reverse. It ponders the relation of man to "the never-setting" and thinks human being from this relation.

With the words "the never-setting" we are translating—as though it were self-evident—the Greek phrase τὸ μὴ δῦνόν ποτε. What do these words signify? Where do we get our information about them? This seems the obvious question to explore, even if the pursuit should lead us far from the saying of Heraclitus. Here, however, and in similar instances, we easily run the risk of searching too far afield. For we presume the phrase is clear enough to warrant an immediate and exclusive search for the sort of thing to which "the never-setting" must, according to Heraclitus' thinking, be attributed. But our inquiry will not take us so far. Nor shall we decide whether the question can be asked in that way. The attempt to render such a decision would fall away once it became clear that the question (to what does Heraclitus ascribe the never-setting?) is superfluous. But how can this be made clear? How can we avoid the danger of inquiring too far afield?

Only if we realize to what degree the phrase τὸ μὴ δῦνόν ποτε gives us quite enough to think about, once we clarify what it says.

The key is τὸ δῦνον. It is related to δύω, which means to envelop, to submerge. Δύειν says: to go into something—the sun goes into the sea, is lost in it. Πρὸς δύνοντος ἡλίου means toward the setting sun, toward evening; νέφεα δῦναι means to sink into the clouds, to disappear behind clouds. Setting, as the Greeks thought of it, takes place as a going into concealment.

We can easily see, if at first only tentatively, that the two main-—because substantial—words with which the fragment begins and ends, τὸ δῦνον and λάθοι, say the Same. But in what sense this is true still remains in question. Meanwhile, we have already gained something when we perceive that the fragment, in its questioning, moves within the realm of concealing. Or do we, as soon as we pursue this line of thinking, lapse into gross error? It seems so, for the fragment names τὸ μὴ δῦνόν ποτε, that which never does set. This is obviously something that never goes into concealment. Concealment is excluded. Of course the fragment would still ask about remaining-concealed. But it questions the possibility of concealment so emphatically that the question amounts to an answer—which rejects the possibility of remaining-concealed. In the form of a simply rhetorical question, the affirmative proposition says: no one can remain concealed before the never-setting. This sounds almost like a maxim.

As soon as we hear the key words τὸ δῦνον and λάθοι in the unbroken unity of the fragment, and no longer extract them as individual terms, it becomes evident that the fragment does not operate in the realm of concealment, but in the utterly opposite sphere. A slight transposition of the construction into the form τὸ μήποτε δῦνον clarifies at once what the fragment is talking about: the never-setting. If we change the negative expression into a completely affirmative one, we then hear for the first time what the fragment means by the "never-setting"—i.e. the ever-rising. In Greek phraseology, this would have to be τὸ ἀεὶ φύον. This turn of speech is not found in Heraclitus. The thinker speaks only of φύσις. In this we hear a primal word of Greek thought. Unexpectedly, then, we get an answer to our question as to what it is whose setting Heraclitus denies.

But can this indication of φύσις as an answer satisfy us, so long as it remains obscure how we are to understand φύσις? And what help are impressive-sounding epithets like "primal word," if the grounds and the abysses [*Gründe und Abgründe*] of Greek thinking so little concern us that we can cloak them in arbitrarily chosen terms borrowed in an utterly thoughtless fashion from our current stock of ideas? If indeed τὸ μήποτε δῦνον is to signify φύσις, then the reference to φύσις will not tell us what τὸ μὴ δῦνόν ποτε is, but the other way around—"the never-setting" urges us to consider how φύσις is experienced as the ever-rising. And what is this latter but what is always-enduring and self-revealing? The saying of the fragment accordingly takes place in the realm of disclosure, not that of concealment.

How, and with respect to what content, must we think the realm of disclosure and disclosing itself, so as not to run the risk of chasing mere terms? The more determined we are to keep from intuitively representing the ever-rising, the never-setting, as some present thing, the more urgent will be the discovery of what it is to which "never-setting" has been given as an attribute.

The desire to know is often praiseworthy; only not when it is rash. But we could scarcely be proceeding more deliberately, not to say fastidiously, when we remain at all times close to the words of the fragment. Have we in fact stayed with them? Or has a barely noticeable transposition of words seduced us to haste, and thus to waste an opportunity for observing something crucial? Apparently so. We transposed τὸ μὴ δῦνόν ποτε into the form τὸ μήποτε δῦνον, and correctly translated μήποτε as "never" and τὸ δῦνον as "that which sets." We considered neither μή, which is stated independently before δῦνον, nor ποτέ, the word that follows δῦνον. We therefore failed to pay attention to a hint proffered us by the negation μή and the adverb ποτέ for a more considered interpretation of δῦνον. Μή is a word of negation. Like οὐκ, it signifies a "not," but in a differense sense. Ὀυκ denies something to whatever is being affected by the negation. Μή, on the other hand, attributes something to whatever comes within its sphere of negation, a refusal, a distancing, a preventing. Μὴ . . . ποτέ says: something does not . . . ever. . . . (What then?) . . . come to pass [*wese*] otherwise than as it comes to pass [*west*].

In Heraclitus' fragment μή and ποτέ bracket δῦνον. Viewed grammatically, the word is a participle. Up until now we have translated it in the apparently more natural nominative meaning. This has served to emphasize the equally natural view that Heraclitus is speaking about the sort of thing that never falls prey to setting. But the negating μὴ . . . ποτε touches on a certain kind of enduring and essential occurring [*Wesen*]. The negation therefore refers to the verbal sense of the participle δῦνον. The same is true of the μή in the ἐόν of Parmenides. The phrase τὸ μὴ δῦνόν ποτε says: the not setting ever.

If we dare for a moment to change the negative phrase back to an affirmative one again, then it becomes clear that Heraclitus thinks the ever-rising, not something to which rising is qualitatively attributed, nor the totality affected by the rising. Rather, he thinks the rising, and only this. The ever and always-enduring rising is named in the thoughtfully spoken word φύσις. We must translate it with the unfamiliar but fitting term "upsurgence," corresponding to the more common "emergence."

Heraclitus thinks the never-setting. In Greek thinking, this is the never-going-into-concealment. In what domain, therefore, does the saying of the fragment take place? According to its sense, it speaks of concealment—i.e. it speaks of never going into concealment. At the same time, the saying directly signifies the always-enduring rising, the ever and always-enduring disclosure. The phrase τὸ μὴ δῦνόν ποτε, the not setting ever, means both revealing *and* concealing—not as two different occurrences merely jammed together, but as one and the

Same. If we pay strict attention to this fact, then we are prevented from carelessly putting τὴν φύσιν in place of τὸ μὴ δῦνόν ποτε. Or is that still possible, perhaps even inevitable? In the latter case, however, we must no longer think of φύσις simply as rising. At bottom, it never means that anyhow. No less a figure than Heraclitus says so, clearly and enigmatically at once. Fragment 123 reads:

Φύσις κρύπτεσθαι φιλεῖ.

Whether the translation "the essence of things likes to hide" even remotely points toward the realm of Heraclitean thinking will not be further discussed here. Perhaps we should not attribute such a commonplace to Heraclitus, even apart from the fact that an "essence of things" first became a matter for thought after Plato. We must heed something else: φύσις and κρύπτεσθαι, rising (self-revealing) and concealing, are named in their closest proximity. This might seem strange at first glance. For if φύσις as rising turns away from, or indeed against, something, then it is κρύπτεσθαι, self-concealing. But Heraclitus is thinking both in closest proximity. Indeed their nearness is explicitly mentioned. Nearness is defined by φιλεῖ. Self-revealing loves self-concealing. What is this supposed to mean? Does rising seek out concealment? Where then must concealment be—and in what sense of "be?" Or does φύσις merely have some kind of sporadically appearing predilection for being a self-concealing, just for a change, rather than a rising? Does the fragment say that rising willingly changes into self-concealing, so that now the one, now the other holds sway? By no means. This interpretation misses the meaning of φιλεῖ, wherein the relation between φύσις and κρύπτεσθαι is named. The interpretation forgets, above all, that decisive matter which the fragment gives us as food for thought: the way in which rising occurs essentially as self-revealing. If, in discussing φύσις, we dare use the expression "occur essentially" [*wesen*], φύσις does not mean "essence" [*das Wesen*], the ὅ τι, the "what" of things. Neither here nor in Fragments 1 and 112, where he uses the form κατὰ φύσιν, does Heraclitus speak of it. The fragment does not think φύσις as the essence of things, but rather thinks the essential presencing (verbal) [*Wesen*], of φύσις.

113

Rising as such is already inclined toward self-closing. The former is concealed in the latter. Κρύπτεσθαι is, as self-concealing, not a mere self-closing but a sheltering in which the essential possibility of rising is preserved—to which rising as such belongs. Self-concealing guarantees self-revealing its true nature [*Wesen*]. In self-concealing, inversely, what reigns is the restraint of the inclination to self-revealing. What would a self-concealing be if it did not restrain itself in its tendency toward rising?

And so φύσις and κρύπτεσθαι are not separated from each other, but mutually inclined toward each other. They are the Same. In such an inclination each first bestows upon the other its proper nature. This inherently reciprocal favoring is the essence of φιλεῖν and of φιλία. In this inclination by which rising and self-concealing lean toward each other the full essence of φύσις consists.

Therefore the translation of Fragment 123, φύσις κρύπτεσθαι φιλεῖ, could run: "Rising (out of self-concealing) bestows favor upon self-concealing."

Still, we are thinking φύσις superficially if we think it as merely rising and letting rise, and if we continue to attribute qualities of any kind to it. By doing that we overlook what is decisive: the fact that self-revealing not only never dispenses with concealing, but actually needs it, in order to occur essentially in the way it occurs [*Wesen, west*] as dis-closing. Only when we think φύσις in this sense may we say τὴν φύσιν instead of τὸ μὴ δῦνόν ποτε.

Both names designate the realm which the reciprocal intimacy of revealing and concealing founds and governs. Within this intimacy is hidden the uniqueness and oneness of Ἕν——the One—which early thinkers presumably beheld in the wealth of its simplicity, which has remained closed to posterity. Τὸ μὴ δῦνόνποτε, "the never going into concealment," never falls prey to concealment only to be dissolved in it, but remains committed to self-concealing, because as the never-going-*into* . . . it is always a rising-*out-of* concealment. For Greek thinking, κρύπτεσαι, though unuttered, is said in τὸ μὴ δῦνόν ποτε, and φύσις is thereby named in its full character, which is governed by the φιλία between revealing and self-concealing.

Perhaps the φιλία of φιλεῖν in Fragment 123 and the ἁρμονίη ἀφανής in Fragment 54 are the Same—granted that the jointure thanks to which revealing and concealing are mutually joined must remain the invisible of all invisibles, since it bestows shining on whatever appears.

The reference to φύσις, φιλία, ἁρμονίη has diminished the vagueness in which τὸ μὴ δῦνόν ποτε, "the never in any case setting," was first heard. But it is difficult to suppress any longer the wish that instead of this explanation of unconcealing and concealing which has no images and no fixed place, some clear information might surface, indicating just where the phrase we have identified properly belongs. We arrive too late with this question, of course. Why? Because τὸ μὴ δῦνόν ποτε names the realm of all realms for early thinking. It is not, however, the highest genus which subordinates different species of realms to it. It is the abode wherein every possible "whither" of a belonging-to rests. Thus the realm, in the sense of μὴ δῦνόν ποτε is unique by virtue of the extent of its gathering reach. Everything that belongs in the event of a rightly experienced revealing grows upward and together (*concrescit*) in this realm. It is the absolutely concrete. But how can this realm be represented as concrete on the basis of the foregoing abstract expositions? This question appears justified only as long as we fail to see that we must not precipitously assault Heraclitus' thought with distinctions like "concrete" and "abstract," "sensuous" and "nonsensuous," "perceptible" and "imperceptible." That they are and have long been current among us does not guarantee their supposedly unlimited importance. It could very well happen that Heraclitus, precisely when he utters a word which names something perceptible is just then thinking what is absolutely imperceptible. Thus it becomes obvious how little we profit from such distinctions.

According to our interpretation, we can replace τὸ μὴ δῦνόν ποτε with τὸ ἀεὶ φύον on two conditions. We must think φύσις from self-concealing, and we must think φύον as a verb. A search for the word ἀείφυον in Heraclitus proves fruitless. We find instead the word ἀείζωον, ever-living, in Fragment 30. The verb "to live" speaks in the largest, uttermost, and inmost significance, which Nietzsche too, in his note from 1885/86, was thinking when he said: " 'Being'—we have no conception of it other than as 'life.'—How can something dead 'be'? " (*Will to Power*, no. 582).

How must we understand our word "life," if we accept it as a faithful translation for the Greek word ζῆν? In ζῆν, ζάω the root ζα– speaks. It is, of course, impossible to conjure up the Greek meaning of "life" from this sound. But we do notice that the Greek language, above all in the speech of Homer and Pindar, uses words like ζάθεος, ζαμενής, ζάπυρος. Linguistics explains that ζα– signifies an intensification. Ζάθεος accordingly means "most divine," "very holy"; ζαμενής, "very forceful"; ζάπυρος, "most fiery." But this "intensification" means neither a mechanical nor a dynamic increase. Pindar calls various locales, mountains, meadows, the banks of a river, ζάθεος, especially when he wants to say that the gods, the shining ones who cast their gaze about, often permitted themselves actually to be seen here. They came to presence by appearing here. These locales are especially holy because they arise purely to allow the appearing of the shining one. So too does ζαμενής mean that which allows the imminent advance of the storm to billow up in its full presencing.

Za- signifies the pure letting-rise within appearing, gazing upon, breaking in upon, and advancing, and all their ways. The verb ζῆν means rising into the light. Homers says, ζῆν καὶ ὁρᾶν φάος ἠελίοιο, "to live, and this means to see the light of the sun." The Greek ζῆν, ζωή, ζῷον must not be interpreted in either a zoological or a broader biological sense. What is named in the Greek ζῷον lies so far from any biologically conceived animality that the Greeks could even call their gods ζῷα. How so? Those who cast their gaze about are those who rise into view. The gods do not experience as animals do. But animality does belong to ζῆν in a special sense. The rising of animals into the open remains closed and sealed in itself in a strangely captivating way. Self-revealing and self-concealing in the animal are one in such a way that human speculation practically runs out of alternatives when it rejects mechanistic views of animality—which are always feasible—as firmly as it avoids anthropomorphic interpretations. Because the animal does not speak, self-revealing and self-concealing, together with their unity, possess a wholly different life-essence [*Lebe-Wesen*] with animals.

But ζωή and φύσις say the same: ἀείζωον means ἀείφυον, which means τὸ μὴ δῦνόν ποτε.

In Fragment 30, the word ἀείζωον follows πῦρ, fire, less as a qualifier than as a separate name which begins the saying anew and which says how the fire is to be thought—as ever-enduring rising. With the word "fire" Heraclitus names that which οὔτε τις θεῶν οὔτε ἀνθρώπων ἐποίησεν, "that which neither any of the gods nor any mortal brought forth," what on the contrary always already rests in itself before gods and men as φύσις, what abides in itself and thus preserves all coming. But this is the κόσμος. We say "world," and think it improperly so long as we represent it exclusively, or even primarily, after the fashion of cosmology or philosophy of nature.

World is enduring fire, enduring rising in the full sense of φύσις. Though we are speaking of an eternal world-conflagration here, we must not first imagine a world which is independent and is then set ablaze and consumed by some ever-burning torch. Rather, the world-ing of world, τὸ πῦρ, τὸ ἀείζωον, τὸ μὴ δῦνόν ποτε, are all the Same. Therefore, the essence of the fire which Heraclitus *thinks* is not as transparently obvious as the image of a glowing flame might suggest. We need only heed ordinary usage, which speaks the word πῦρ from diverse perspectives and thereby points toward the essential fullness of what is intimated in the thoughtful saying of the word.

Πῦρ names the sacrificial fire, the oven's fire, the campfire, but also the glow of a torch, the scintillation of the stars. In "fire," lighting, glowing, blazing, soft shining hold sway and that which opens an expanse in brightness. In "fire," however, consuming, welding, cauterizing, extinguishing also reign. When Heraclitus speaks of fire, he is primarily thinking of the lighting governance, the direction [*das Weisen*] which gives measure and takes it away. According to a fragment in Hippolytus, discovered and convincingly authenticated by Karl Reinhardt (*Hermes* 77 [1942], 1 ff.) τὸ πῦρ is for Heraclitus also τὸ φρόνιμον, the meditative [*das Sinnende*]. It indicates the direction of everything, and lays before everything where it belongs. The meditative fire which lays before gathers all together and secures it in its essence. The meditative fire is the gathering which lays everything there before us (into presencing). Τὸ Πῦρ is ὁ Λόγος. Its meditating is the heart, i.e. the lighting-sheltering expanse, of the world. In a multiplicity of different names—φύσις, πῦρ, λόγος, ἁρμονίη, πόλεμος, ἔρις, (φιλία), ἕν—Heraclitus thinks the essential fullness of the Same.

From beginning to end and back again this list refers to the phrase that begins Fragment 16: τὸ μὴ δῦνόνποτε, the not setting ever. What is named in it must be heard in consonance with all those fundamental words of Heraclitean thinking to which we have referred.

In the meantime, we have seen that never entering into concealment is the enduring rising out of self-concealing. In this way does the world fire glow and shine and meditate. If we think it as lighting, this includes not only the brilliance, but also the openness wherein everything, especially the reciprocally related, comes into shining. Lighting is therefore more than illuminating, and also more than laying bare. Lighting is the meditatively gathering bringing-before into the open. It is the bestowal of presencing.

The event of lighting is the world. The meditatively gathering lighting which brings into the open is revealing; it abides in self-concealing. Self-concealing belongs to it as that which finds its essence in revealing, and which therefore cannot ever be a mere going into concealment, never a setting.

Πῶς ἄν τις λάθοι; "how then could anyone remain concealed?" the fragment asks, with reference to the forementioned τὸ μὴ δῦνόν ποτε, which stands in the accusative. In translating, we make it the object of a preposition in the dative case—"How could anyone remain hidden before it, that is, before the lighting?" Without giving a reason, the *form* of the question rejects such a possibility. The reason must already lie in what is questioned itself. All too quickly we are prepared to bring it forward: since the never-setting, the lighting, sees and notices everything, nothing can hide before it. But there is no mention of seeing and noticing in the fragment. Above all, however, the fragment does not say πῶς ἄν τι, "how could *something* . . .?" but πῶς ἄν τις, "how could some*one* . . . ?" According to the fragment, the lighting is in no way related to whatever just happens to be present. Who is meant by the τίς? Our first impulse is to think of a human person, especially since the question is posed by a mortal and addressed to human beings. But because a thinker is speaking here, particularly that thinker who abides near Apollo and Artemis, his speaking could be a dialogue with those who cast their gaze on things, and could co-signify in τίς "anyone," the gods. We are strengthened in this surmise by Fragment 30, which says, οὔτε τις θεῶν οὔτε ἀνθρώπων. Similarly, Fragment 53, often cited, but incompletely for the most part, mentions mortals and immortals together when it says πόλεμος, the setting-apart-from-each-other (the lighting), manifests some of those present as gods, others as men, and brings some forward into appearance as slaves and others as free. This says: the enduring lighting lets gods and men come to presence in unconcealment in such a way that none of them could remain concealed; not because he is observed by someone, but because—and only because—each comes to presence. The presencing of gods, however, is other than that of men. As δαίμονες, θεάοντες, the gods are those who look into the lighting of what is present, which concerns mortals after their own fashion, as they let what is present lie before them in its presence and as they continue to take heed of it.

The lighting, therefore, is no mere brightening and lightening. Because presencing means to come enduringly forward from concealment to unconcealment, the revealing-concealing lighting is concerned with the presencing of what is present. Fragment 16, however, does not speak of just any and every something, τί, which could come to presence, but unequivocally and only of τίς, someone among gods and men. Thus the fragment seems to name only a limited range of what is present. Or, rather than limit us to a particular realm of what is present, does the fragment perhaps contain something exceptional which shatters limits and concerns the realm of all realms? Is its exceptional character such that the fragment seeks to know what tacitly collects and embraces also those present beings which are not to be counted as among the regions of gods and men, but which are nevertheless human and divine in another sense—present beings such as plants and animals, mountains, seas, and stars?

But in what else could the exceptional character of gods and men consist, if not in the fact that precisely they in their relation to the lighting can never remain concealed? Why is it that they cannot? Because their relation to the lighting is nothing other than the lighting itself, in that this relation gathers men and gods into the lighting and keeps them there.

The lighting not only illuminates what is present, but gathers it together and secures it in advance in presencing. But of what sort is the presencing of gods and men? They are not only illuminated in the lighting, but are also enlightened from it and toward it. Thus they can, in *their* way, accomplish the lighting (bring it to the fullness of its essence) and thereby protect it. Gods and men are not only lighted by a light—even if a supersensible one—so that they can never hide themselves from it in darkness; they are luminous in their essence. They are alight [*er-lichtet*]; they are appropriated into the event of lighting, and therefore never concealed. On the contrary, they are re-vealed, thought in still another sense. Just as those who are far distant belong to the distance, so are the revealed—in the sense now to be thought—entrusted to the lighting that keeps and shelters them. According to their essence, they are trans-posed [*ver-legt*] to the concealing of the mystery, gathered together, belonging to the Λόγος in ὁμολογεῖν (Fragment 50).

Did Heraclitus intend his question as we have just been discussing it? Was what this discussion has said within the range of his concepts? Who knows? Who can say? But perhaps the fragment, independently of Heraclitus' own representational range, says the sort of thing our tentative discussion has put forward. The fragment does say it—provided a thoughtful dialogue may bring it to speak. The fragment says it, and leaves it unuttered. The paths that lead through the region of the unuttered remain questions, questions which always evoke only such things as were manifested long ago on those paths under diverse disguises.

The fundamentally interrogative character of the fragment indicates that Heraclitus is contemplating the revealing-concealing lighting, the world fire, in its scarcely perceptible relation to those who are en-lightened in accord with their essence, and who therefore hearken to and belong to the lighting in an exceptional way.

Or does the fragment speak out of an experience of thinking which has already weighed every step? Might Heraclitus' question only be saying that evidently there is no way possible for the relation of the world fire to gods and men to be other than this: gods and men belong in the lighting not only as lighted and viewed, but also as invisible, bringing the lighting with them in their own way, preserving it and handing it down in its endurance?

In this case the fragment, with its questioning, could give voice to a thoughtful wonder, which stands expectantly [*verhofft*] before that relation wherein the lighting takes the essence of gods and men unto itself. The questioning saying would then correspond to what is ever and again worthy of wonder and is preserved in its worth by wonder.

It is impossible to estimate how much and how clearly Heraclitus' thinking presaged the realm of all realms. That the fragment moves within the realm of the lighting cannot be doubted as soon as we consider ever more clearly this one matter: the beginning and the end of the fragment name revealing and concealing—particularly with respect to their interconnection. We do not even require a separate reference to Fragment 50, in which the revealing-concealing gathering is identified as being entrusted to mortals in such a way that their essence unfolds in this: their correspondence or noncorrespondence to the Λόγος.

We are too quick to believe that the mystery of what is to be thought always lies distant and deeply hidden under a hardly penetrable layer of strangeness. On the contrary, it has its essential abode in what is near by, which approaches what is coming into presence and preserves what has drawn near. The presencing of the near is too close for our customary mode of representational thought—which exhausts itself in securing what is present—to experience the governance of the near, and without preparation to think it adequately. Presumably, the mystery that beckons in what is to be thought is nothing other than essentially what we have attempted to suggest in the name the "lighting." Everyday opinion, therefore, self-assuredly and stubbornly bypasses the mystery. Heraclitus knew this. Fragment 72 runs:

ὧι μάλιστα διηνεκῶς ὁμιλοῦσι Λόγωι, τούτωι διαφέρονται, καὶ οἷς καθ᾽ ἡμέραν ἐγκυροῦσι, ταῦτα αὐτοῖς ξένα φαίνεται.

From that to which for the most part they are bound and by which they are thoroughly sustained, the Λόγος, from that they separate themselves; and it becomes manifest: whatever they daily encounter remains foreign (in its presencing) to them.*

Mortals are irrevocably bound to the revealing-concealing gathering which lights everything present in its presencing. But they turn from the lighting, and turn only toward what is present, which is what immediately concerns them in their everyday commerce with each other. They believe that this trafficking in what is present by itself creates for them a sufficient familiarity with it. But it nonetheless remains foreign to them. For they have no inkling of what they have been entrusted with: presencing, which in its lighting first allows what is present to come to appearance. Λόγος, in whose lighting they come and go, remains concealed from them, and forgotten.

The more familiar to them everything knowable becomes, the more foreign it is to them—without their being able to know this. They would become aware of all this if only they would ask: how could anyone whose essence belongs to the lighting ever withdraw from receiving and protecting the lighting? How could he, without immediately discovering that the everyday can seem quite ordinary to him only because this ordinariness is guilty of forgetting what initially brings even the apparently self-evident into the light of what is present?

Everyday opinion seeks truth in variety, the endless variety of novelties which are displayed before it. It does not see the quiet gleam (the gold) of the mystery that everlastingly shines in the simplicity of the lighting. Heraclitus says (Fragment 9):

ὄνους σύρματ' ἂν ἑλέσθαι μᾶλλον ἢ χρυσόν.

"Asses choose hay rather than gold."

---

*Diels-Kranz (I, 167) translate, " . . . from the Meaning with which for the most part they go about (from that which governs the totality), from that they separate themselves, and the things they encounter every day seem strange to them." A more fluent translation appears in the excellent French collection by Jean Brun, *Héraclite, ou le philosophe de l'éternel retour* (Paris: Seghers, 1965), p. 188: "However closely united they are to the Logos which governs the world, they separate themselves from it, etc."—TR.

But the golden gleam of the lighting's invisible shining cannot be grasped, because it is not itself something grasping. Rather, it is the purely appropriating event [*das reine Ereignen*]. The invisible shining of the lighting streams from wholesome self-keeping in the self-restraining preservation of destiny. Therefore the shining of the lighting is in itself at the same time a self-veiling—and is in that sense what is most obscure.

Heraclitus is called ὁ Σκοτεινός. He will also retain this name in the future. He is the Obscure, because he thinks questioningly into the lighting.

Glossary

das Abendland	the West
das Abend-Land	the land of evening
abgehen	to decline, depart
der Abgrund	abyss
die Abwesenheit	absence
achten	to heed, pay attention to
in-die-Acht-nehmen	(νοεῖν) to take heed of
die Ankunft	advent, arrival
der Anspruch	claim
anwesen	to come to presence
das Anwesen	(ἐόν) presencing
das Anwesende	(ἐόντα) what is present
die Anwesenheit	presence
das Aufgehen	rising
das Aussehen	(εἶδος, ἰδέα) form, outer appearance
das Beharren	persistence
sich beharren auf	to insist on, persist in
beisammen-vor-liegen-Lassen	(λέγειν) to let-lie-together-before
der Bereich	realm, domain
bergen	to shelter, secure, conceal
entbergen	to disclose, reveal
das Sichentbergen	(φύσις) self-revealing
verbergen	to conceal, hide
das Sichverbergen	(κρύπτεσθαι) self-concealing
die Beständigung	continuance
der Brauch	(χρεών) usage, use, need, custom
brauchen	to need, use, need to use

bruchen	*(frui)* to brook, enjoy, have usufruct
das Denken	(νοεῖν) thinking
andenken	remember, recall, recollect
bedenken	think of, consider
das Denkwürdige	what is worthy of thought, the thought-provoking
das zu-Denkende	what is to be thought, what is for thinking
dichten	poetize
dunkel	(σκοτεινός) obscure, dark
eigentlich	proper, genuine
eigens	expressly, explicitly
einholen	to collect
das Einzig-Eine	('Εν) the unique one
einen	to unify, unite
das Entbergen	disclosure
entlang	(κατά) along the lines of
ereignen	to appropriate
sich ereignen	to come to pass
das Ereignis	the event
die Frühe	dawn, early times
das Fug	(δίκη) order
das Un-Fug	(ἀδικία) disorder
die Fuge	jointure
die Un-Fuge	disjunction
fügen	to join
verfügen	to conjoin, enjoin
die Gegend	expanse, region, province
das Geheiss	call, gesture
gehören	belong
hören	hear
hörchen	hearken
das Gehör	attunement
ein Gesagtes	something said

ein Gespräch	conversation
ein Gesprochenes	something spoken, utterance
die Geschichte	history
die Historie	historiography
das Geschick	destiny, destining, Fate
das Geschick des Seins	the destiny(-ing) of Being
das Gesicht	(ἰδέα) aspect
das Gleiche	what is identical or alike
der Graben	abyss
der Grund	ground, reason (for)
die Helle	brightness, brilliance
die Herkunft	arrival, emergence, origin
die Hut	protection
je-weilen	to linger awhile
das je-weilige Anwesende	what lingers awhile in presence; that which for the time being is
das je und je Weilige	what in each case lingers
lassen	to let
bei-sammen-vor-liegen-Lassen	to let-lie-together-before
loslassen	to release
legen	(λέγειν) to lay
die lesende Lege	the Laying that gathers
lesen	to gather, read
die Lese	the vintage, gathering
die Auslese	the selection
das Erlesene	the to-be-selected
lichten	to clear, lighten, illuminate
die Lichtung	the clearing, lighting
die lichtende-bergende-Versammlung	the gathering that clears and shelters
liegen	to lie
massgebend	definitive, standard
die Nähe	nearness, proximity
der Ort	(τόπος) place

die Ortschaft	abode
	'
das Rätsel	riddle, enigma
das Rätselwort	enigmatic key word
das Recht	(δίκη) right, justice
das Unrecht	(ἀδικία) wrong, injustice
der Ruch	reck
ruchlos	reckless
die Rücksicht	consideration
rücksichtlos	inconsiderate
die Sage	the saying (verbal)
sammeln	to gather
sich sammeln	to assemble
die Sammlung	the gathering, coordination
die Versammlung	the assembly(-ing)
der Satz	sentence, proposition
schätzen	to esteem
scheinen	to shine, appear
der Schein	shining, appearance
das Erscheinen	appearance (verbal)
der Anschein	semblance, apparition
der Vorschein	prominence, appearance
schicken	to send
sich schicken	to devote oneself to, dispatch oneself toward
schickliches	appropriate, fitting
geschickt werden	to become skillful
der Schick	calling, vocational skill
das Geschickliche	Fate, the fateful itself
geschicklich	fateful
das Geschick	destiny, destining, Fate
die Schickung	dispensation
sein	(εἶναι) to be
das Sein	(ἐόν) Being
das Seiende	(ἐόντα) being(s)
das Seiende-im-Ganzen	being-in-totality
das Selbe	(τὸ αὐτό) the Same
die Sprache	language, speech

der Spruch	fragment, saying
Strafe und Busse	recompense and penalty
übersetzen	translate, cross over
untergehen	(δΰνον) to go down, set
das niemals Untergehende	the never-setting
die Unverborgenheit	unconcealment
die Verborgenheit	concealment
verborgenbleiben	to remain concealed
vergessen	(ἐπιλανθάνεσθαι) to forget
die Vergessenheit des Seins	the oblivion of Being
das Vernehmen	apprehension, perception
die Versammlung	assembly, gathering
die Verwindung	the surmounting (of)
das Vorhandene	something at hand
der Vorschein	prominence, appearance
in-den-Vorschein-bringen	to bring forward into view
zum Vorschein kommen	to come forward into appearance, to come to the fore
das Vorstellen	representational thought
wahren	*(die Wahrheit)* to preserve
die Wahrnis	preservation
walten	to hold sway, reign, rule, dominate
die Weile	the while
weilen	to linger
wesen	to occur essentially, presence
das Wesen	essence, essential being
die Zusammengehörigkeit	belonging-together
die Zuteilung	(Μοῖρα) apportionment, allotment
die Zwiefalt	the duality, twofold (of Being and beings)
die Entfaltung der Zwiefalt	the unfolding of the twofold